No Matter What

Kathryn Merriam

ISBN 978-1-64468-665-2 (Paperback)
ISBN 978-1-64468-666-9 (Digital)

Covenant Books, Inc.
11661 Hwy 707
Murrells Inlet, SC 29576
www.covenantbooks.com

1

The End

The one place where she never wanted to set foot again. Not after what happened before. She promised herself that she wouldn't do it again, that she would never need to again. But God had other plans. So there she was, in a hospital room, her life on the line, even though he was hooked up to the machines. He was the one with a bandage on his head. He was the one with the missing right leg. But she couldn't move. She couldn't even breathe. Nor did she want to.

She had said yes. Yes, he could go serve in the military. Not that it was up to her really, but he had asked. And she said yes; she would wait for him. And then, there he was on one knee. And she said yes again. And then once more when they made promises to each other and to God. But without fully realizing it, she had also said yes to pouring her heart out in worried prayer every day, crying herself to sleep most nights, and living with a question she could never answer. Only He could. But He never seemed to answer that question.

"Love," she paused as she choked on sobs and squeezed the hand she had not released since she allowed herself to be in the same room as him, "I'm right here. Always." It had been that way ever since April 22, 2015, just three years and eight months prior. He was twenty-two. She was twenty-one. And both of them decided to take the evening off from schoolwork to enjoy time away from their apartments, away from responsibility, away from life. But first, it was imperative, for both of them, to get pizza.

He got there a second before she did, but he took an extra few seconds to hold the door open for her. Wearing black skinny jeans and her *Top Gun* t-shirt, she clasped her hands together in front of her, bit her lip, and looked down as she entered. There may have been a curtsy in there too, but she doesn't like to talk about that part. Lucky for her, I do.

"Thank you." Without looking him in the eyes, she remained polite.

"Uh...oh! You're welcome." His gray shirt accentuated his shoulders, and his blue jeans framed his legs well, not that she would admit to taking any notice. As she continued to look down, she missed his blonde hair and green eyes. Breathing in the smell of fresh pizza, particularly melted cheese, she curved around the eight people waiting and found her way to the end of the line.

The bell above the door rang as it closed behind him, but his eyes did not move from off of her face, at least the part of her face he could see. He didn't miss the peeking smile or the button nose on her face, but he wished she would look up. His eyes remained fixed on her, glued in place as if he could not move them. Well, he didn't want to. So he made his way to stand behind her in line.

"Go ahead." She gestured for him to take a spot in front of her in line, but he was raised to be a gentleman, so that just wouldn't do.

"Uh, no. That's okay. I will just wait behind you." Her head cocked to the side as she finally looked up to meet his eyes. And there they were.

No longer was he in Little Caesars in southern California. His mind took him back home, where he came from. And she was there too. He could picture it—the two of them going everywhere together, doing everything together. Their favorite thing to do was to picture an ocean, or any lake they could dream of, and to walk along it, even push each other into the water. But most of the time, they just talked, about the future mainly, about their hopes and dreams. And then she did it: the one thing he knew he would never forget. She looked up at him with eyes that he imagined reflected the most perfect and purest ocean. Crystal blue danced around the outside, but an occasional sliver of green made its way into the canvas as a gold tint encompassed her inner eye. He had seen those irises so many times before, but not quite like this, not with this beauty, this intensity.

"Uh…what?" He noticed that she had stepped closer to him and kept the smile on her face. Her teeth may not be sparkling white, but they were perfect nonetheless.

"I thought I was the only one to get lost into such deep thoughts." Her giggle made his heart soar. Now, without a doubt, he knew. He knew he had found her. But did she remember?

Heavenly Father, I found her. You helped me to find her, and here she is. Right in front of me. Please, please help her to remember me. Please.

"Uh, no." He let out a chuckle. "Apparently not. I haven't done that before." He let the right side of his mouth lift just a smidge, and she could see his crooked bottom teeth. "But that was before I met you." She laughed, and his heart leapt once again. It was her. Oh, he so knew it was her! And she was currently looking at him with furrowed eyebrows as her eyes danced with humor.

"Did you say something else?" He felt his face heat up. If even just a little. Ignoring the people around them, they remained in place, only three feet away from the counter and right next to the four empty chairs.

"I asked if you are sure you don't want to go first," she smiled and added, "multiple times."

"I'm sorry. I don't mean to be rude."

"I know." She carried an upbeat tone that started to cascade past his barriers, as if they weren't already down.

"You do?"

She stood a little taller and leaned a little closer. "Yes." She rose up on her tippy toes and landed softly on the ground while biting back a smile.

"And how do you know?" He cocked one eyebrow.

"Because…" But then she didn't go on, for way too long.

"Because?" He couldn't wait.

"Are you in line?" A woman and her son stood behind them in line.

Briefly glancing at her before turning to the young mother before him, he replied, "Uh, no, not anymore. Sorry."

As others behind them followed suit, she apologized as well, looked at him, and gestured toward a spot along the wall in between the edge of the dark counter and the sunset wall.

"Because you opened the door for me." He froze. She saw the questions fill his gaze, so she proceeded to explain. Much to his appreciation. "Men who open doors for others are special men of God." Did she just call him a man? Oh, he liked the sound of that, very much. His chest puffed out a bit more as he stood a little taller.

"Uh, thank you."

"Do you always use that word when you talk to people?"

"Uh, what word?" She tried and failed to hold in her laughter. It got away from her, and before he knew it, he joined in. Moments later, though, he paused.

He could picture the two of them laughing together at whatever joke the other had made. And they would stay that way for several minutes until one of them grasped the other's shoulder as if to retrieve oxygen. Sometimes she would even laugh so hard she began to wheeze. They fed off each other's words, thoughts, laughter; they thrived on each other's breath in a way very few ever did.

Sorry, Father, I got a little distracted. And I know I just said this, but I know: this is her. I have found her, Dad! You helped me to find her! And here she is! Thank You. Thank You for helping me keep my promise. In the name of Jesus Christ, amen.

And there she was, in Little Caesars, still standing in front of him, with that same look on her face. That look that said she knew what he was thinking.

"I, uh, sorry, guess I got lost in thought again."

"I know." This time, he just smiled. Because she knew too. It was what she said to him every time she knew something before he did, which he had a feeling would happen a lot.

Before she could continue, he laughed and quickly added, "I know you know." He then proceeded to wrap his arms around her and squeeze. She held onto him like she would never let go.

"Anja?" She looked up to see a man dressed in what looked like a doctor's uniform standing in the doorway. Probably the doctor. "May I come in?"

"Uh, yes, yes, you may. I just—" She didn't know how to finish that sentence.

"He is looking better today." She laughed, but there was no humor behind it. The doctor must have sensed it because he immediately continued, "We are going to take the tube out today. He can breathe on his own now." She looked away from the doctor to stare at him—her SJ, the one who promised he would find her, no matter what. And he did. He found her three years ago, and they had been inseparable since. Until that day that changed everything. No matter how much she didn't want to admit it, the gap between them felt like a gulf, a gulf that would take her too, if it took SJ.

"Anja?"

"Sorry, Doctor...?" She couldn't look him in the eyes; she didn't want to see what they weren't telling her.

"Dr. Anderson. We've met before, remember?" She did. She remembered. He was the one who told her that his future didn't look good. He was the one who told her that they didn't expect him to make it until tomorrow, which happened three weeks ago. He was the one who held her up before she collapsed onto the hard tile floor. He was the one who sat with her in the waiting room, reciting terms and numbers and names that she didn't remember, that she didn't care about. Because all she remembered was "Your husband...can't...breathe...lost his leg..." That is all she needed to know. No, it was more than she wanted to know. But those words rang in her head more than anything else. And all she wanted was for it to all go away. She only knew one person who could do that. So, for the sixth time that day, she asked Him.

Dear Father, please, take this from me. Take it away. Please help things go back to the way they were. Before the war. Before the pain. God, please. I need You. In the name of Your Beloved Son, Jesus Christ, amen.

Anja, I am right here.

"Really?" She didn't realize she had said it out loud until the doctor abruptly stopped what he was doing and looked at her. "Sorry."

She waved, hoping he would understand what she was trying to convey. But he was no longer looking at her. Instead, he was taking the tube out, the oxygen tube. She stood up faster than she ever had before, still holding her husband's hand. "Wait, Dr. Anderson! You can't do—" She stopped.

For the first time in several weeks, it finally happened: she felt her heart beat. Steady. *Thump-thump*. Consistent. *Thump-thump*. Rhythmic. *Thump-thump*. Independent. *Thump-thump*. Because so was his.

Dear Heavenly Father, thank You. Thank You. She sat against the back of the chair that had become her new place of residence and squeezed her husband's hand.

God, I am sorry. I am sorry for forgetting that You are in charge, that You are the head of this family, that You alone are my Creator. You are his Creator. Only You can give SJ life, and You have. And he is still here with me. I need him, Father, You know that. So, thank You, Father. Thank You. In the name of my Savior, Jesus Christ, amen.

"Anja!" Dr. Anderson was no longer the only other person in the hospital room. There were two other nurses and a third one she could see running toward his room. A familiar-looking machine rested on the other side of SJ's bed. The machine that pumps electricity into someone whose heart has stopped, into someone who is no longer breathing on one's own.

Thump-thump. She couldn't do it. *Thump.* Not again. She clung to herself as the male nurse carried her away from her husband. *Thump.* Her dead husband.

2

The Promise

No matter how much she hoped he would, she knew he couldn't keep his second promise—the one that tried to convince both of them he would come home to her. Not many husbands like hers did. Even though SJ pleaded with Anja to keep living life to the fullest, even though SJ tried to convince her that everything he did was for God and for her, even though SJ promised that he would come back to her, it hurt. Not a single part of her was free. Not a single part of her still knew what it was like to live a normal life, a life with him in it. Yes, she had her dream job of planning weddings, but that wasn't enough. She volunteered at the nearby homeless shelter, devoted her time to her church, to her God, but it still wasn't complete. It wasn't home.

It all started by the lake. Set apart by a small forest behind her parents' house, the lake became their getaway spot—a time and place to remove themselves from the world, from school, and, yes, sometimes even from his parents.

The seafoam green rim of the lake carried their attention out to the crystal surface water. Surrounded by cattails and green grass that looked like it came straight out of a painting, the lake always seemed to be accompanied by a perfect breeze. It wasn't strong enough to be overpowering, but rather, it allowed the cattails, the water, and the grass to dance in perfect harmony, creating their own song with an unforgettable tune. Their favorite time was at sunset, so when needed, and even just on a whim, SJ and Anja would walk together out to the lake just as the sun started to gracefully descend beneath the horizon. Peach, butter, and rose lights shot across the sky, creating a canvas only truly captured in their memory.

"Don't finish that sentence." She jumped up from her position at his side on the shore of the lake. The ocean-blue hue of her eyes became hidden beneath a shadow that rolled into her gaze. "I know you are not thinking what I think you are."

"Uh… Anja?" his voice squeaked, but both ignored it as he stood to join her.

"What, SJ? How did you expect me to react?" After tucking his hands into the pocket of his jeans, he looked down and away. "We have been dating for eight months, and this is just now coming up in conversation. You were going to graduate in three semesters, but now, all of the sudden, you're changing gears completely?" She crossed her arms in front of her chest.

"Yes." It was barely a whisper.

"I lost my grandfather because of it. My grandmother was so devastated that she"—she stepped away as he reached for her hands—"died of a broken heart, SJ. You know that. All because he went off to the war…" She didn't want to finish.

"And never came home."

"Yes, he never came home." Her taller stance began to slump as he saw the pain being replaced by something he couldn't quite pinpoint. "And now you expect me to live with that uncertainty, the pain of the reminders, the fear that you will never come home when you go off to serve. And I stay here."

"Love, that is not the purpose behind this decision."

"Then what is the reason behind it? Because all I see right now is you leaving me behind," she paused for effect, "and alone." He hung his head and turned to face the lake. After a few moments of silence, he took a deep breath and looked toward the sun.

"Do you remember the day we found each other?"

"Of course, I do, SJ. It was the best day of my life." He smiled in whole-hearted agreement.

"Do you also remember the promise I made to you that day?" She didn't care about the tears that silently fell. She couldn't help it. So she didn't fight him as he reached up, faced her, and used his right thumb to wipe the tears off her face.

"You know I do, SJ. I always have—"

"And always will." He used his left hand to tenderly lift her chin.

"Yes." Another tear threatened to fall, and she let it.

"Have I ever broken a promise?" She leaned her head onto the hand that still resided next to her face.

"No, love, you haven't."

"So, do you really think I would start now?" Before anything else happened, she made up the distance and wrapped her arms around him. She loved being able to curl her arms up along his back as she let her hands rest on his shoulders.

Leaning closer to his ear, she asked, "Do you remember the promise I made to you only moments after you made that promise to me?" Her heart melted as she felt his laugh ripple through his body.

"I do." He paused again to let out another chuckle. "You promised you would never let me go." He chuckled again and this time, she joined him, "Even if that meant holding onto me for eternity." The lightness of his tone seemed to fade as he continued, "You promised you would do whatever it took." She tightened her grip on his back, massaging along his spine.

"Exactly."

"Exactly," he whispered the echo, longing to hold her forever.

"So"—he cringed, knowing what she was going to ask—"how do we both keep the promises we made to each other?"

"We pray about it." She started to laugh.

"I think that you have already done that." Her laugh ended just as quickly as it started. "I just don't know why you did it without me." Before he could speak, she continued, "I know we are not married, or even engaged, but this is a decision that not only impacts you, it impacts us." He made a motion to step back. But just as quickly, she squeezed even tighter.

"Love, I just need to look you in the eyes. I'm not going any-where." Holding back her much-desired response, she let him take a step back, but only a few inches.

"Somethings I need to work out with Him, and Him alone, but that does not mean that I will not go to you about those decisions. We are a team. I know that. And I want that, more than anything, but He and I come first. All of my decisions will go through Him first. Besides, I was going to tell you either way it went, but I only just got a definite answer."

She couldn't look him in the eyes as she replied, "The answer that will send you away from me. The answer that puts your life in danger. The answer—"

"That is from Him, who knows what is best, who loves us more than anyone, and who wants us to be happy and to experience joy." She didn't want to admit that everything he said rang true. She knew that. She just had one question.

"Why?" Once again, he brought her head up so he could look into her ocean eyes, the eyes that he looked forward to seeing every day, the eyes that brought the meaning of life into his soul the second he saw them.

"We don't have to know the *why*. All we need to know is that He is there, that He knows what He is doing, and that we can trust Him with our lives." Again, he was right.

"God is my best friend, love. You know that. And I trust Him with all that I am. I learned that the hard way." He gave her an empa-thetic smile, knowing that she and He had been an inseparable team since she came back after the breakup. "But"—tears started to fall once again, yet this time, she watched them trace his face—"I also love you with all of me, all that I am, and all that I will be." She brought her hands up to cup his face. "You are my love, SJ. My one and only. I gave Him my heart, and He trusted you with it, and that means more to me than you will ever know."

"So?"

"Yes, I will let you serve. I will trust you in His hands. I will give you to Him, but I will be here, waiting for you to come back to me," she closed her eyes, took a deep breath, and then opened them to gaze into the eyes that she had grown to adore, the eyes that unlocked his soul, the eyes she could read like a book, and whispered, "and praying that you will come back to me." Without hesitation, he lifted her and spun her in a circle. And then he squeezed.

There was no more waiting. Not with her. "Uh…marry me!" Wrapped in his arms, she didn't move. She didn't respond. Until she laughed. A good, hearty laugh. He released her ever so slightly. "Anja?"

After allowing herself to catch her breath, she explained, "Oh, SJ. If that is your way of proposing, it will not do. You know it means more to me than that, so if you are going to ask, you need to do it the right way." She let her weight fall onto her right hip as she folded her arms in front of her. SJ responded with a smirk, one that told her he knew exactly what she meant, and that it was her turn to be right.

He dropped down to one knee, pulled the ring out of his pocket, and looked into her eyes. Her arms dropped to her sides.

"Anja Rose Whittle, will you, my love, marry me?"

Just waiting long enough for him to complete the question, she responded by flapping her arms as she attempted to cover her mouth. He saw her tears, and heard her flaps. She had always been animated, and it was just one more thing that he found adorable about her. Once the flapping died down, she confessed, "Yes, Scott James Gensicki, I will marry you!" They embraced with no intention of ever letting go.

After several moments, SJ spoke up, "Can I put the ring on?" Both of them giggled as she admitted she forgot about it. "This is a reminder that my love for you will never ever run out."

She grabbed his hands and looked him in the eyes. "Thank you, SJ."

"Thank you, Anja." She took a second to look at the ring. It was a simple diamond with a floral band to accompany it. No, she didn't know what size diamond, how many carats it was composed of, how much money it cost, but she didn't need to know. All she needed was the man standing before her.

As they left the lake in their dust, Anja exclaimed, "I cannot wait to tell your parents! They are going to be so excited!" He coughed, but not in a way that meant he had something in his lungs.

"Uh… I haven't told them yet."

She folded her hand in his and responded, "I know that, love, since it just happened. So we get to tell them together!" He laughed, a little, and then grew really quiet. Anja stopped walking and turned to face him without letting go of his hand.

"What aren't you telling me?" One look from him, and she knew. He wasn't referring to their engagement. No! He was admitting that he hadn't told them that he was going to leave. And not come back.

3

───◇○ ○◇───

The Prayer

From three to two. Because he left them. It wasn't so he could abandon them. It was so that He could listen to and act on His words. But his mom wouldn't see it that way. He rolled off the bed of his temporary apartment to land softly on his knees—a motion that took years of practice.

Dear Heavenly Father, thank You that the sun is shining. Thank You for such a beautiful day. And thank You for Anja. She is such an important part of my life, and I really want it to stay that way. But, Father, if this is not Your plan, please let me know. I need to know what You want me to do next. I need to know what You want me to do, who You want me to become. I am Yours, in every way. And then he waited.

Son, you know what I want you to do next.

But, Father, that will take me away from her. Am I not supposed to be with her? Yes, I have been looking into it, researching it, meeting with people, but You know that. And You know what I will have to sacrifice, who I will have to sacrifice. Father, in all honesty, I don't think I will be able to leave her.

Oh, my son, you know I would never ask you to do something that you cannot.

Dad, it is more a matter of something that I do not want to do.

I know, My son. But I need you to trust Me.

Father, I do. He hung his head. *I do trust You with all that I am, but...* But what?

15

SJ, I am here with you. And I will be with her. I always have been, and I always will be with both of you.

Father, I cannot let her go. I cannot leave her. What if…

Silence. SJ rested his head on his hands and waited. Moments passed. Still, he waited.

My Son, I am not asking you to let her go.

How not, Father? How are You not asking me to leave her? To abandon her? And my parents? To leave behind everything I have, everything I love?

I sent My Son for you. For her. For everyone. He knows what it is like, for He has experienced the ultimate sacrifice. I am not asking you to give up your loved ones. I am asking you to trust Me. I am asking you to follow Me, My son. Just as He did.

SJ stayed still. The only sound was the wind dancing with the chimes just outside the window.

Father, I will. I will follow You. I will join the United States Marines Corp. I just ask that You please give me the words and the strength that I need to tell—a tear fell down his cheek—*my parents.* He took a deep breath. *In the name of Jesus Christ, amen.*

Silence. But he knew his Father was there, listening, and that He would answer. After all, He was there when he spoke to Anja. But now, it was time to tell his parents.

He walked up to the front door. Its red paint covered most of the surface area with the exception of the Victorian window positioned in the center near the top. He knew he didn't have to knock, but he did anyway.

His mother opened the door and was immediately wrapping her arms around him. It was a traditional custom every time he visited. But this time, he couldn't hug her back.

She broke the embrace, kept her hands on his shoulders, and looked into her son's eyes. He could see the apron she was wearing and smell the cookies she was baking. They were his favorites—double chocolate delights. And it just made everything worse.

"Hello, Mother. Is Dad home?"

She jokingly slapped his shoulder. "Oh, SJ, what is up with all this 'Mother' business? And yes, your father is home. He's in the study. Why?" He didn't respond. She grabbed his hand and led him into the dining room that was only an archway away from the kitchen. When he still didn't respond, she turned around to see tears in his eyes.

"Oh, SJ, honey, what's wrong?" She stroked his hair. "Talk to me!" The pleading in her voice did not go unnoticed; it only hurt that much more. She grabbed his other hand and held them, waiting for him to be ready. "SJ..." SJ just squeezed her hands, pleading with her to let him explain. After gaining his composure, he looked into her hazel eyes.

"Mom, do you remember that day when I came home from school crying?" She silently nodded.

"Of course, I do. It was the only day I have seen you cry." She angled her head, lowered her eyebrows, and exposed her right dimple as she tenderly lifted the right side of her mouth. "Besides today."

"Do you remember why I was crying?" She gave a quick laugh.

"I do. You said that you were disobedient and that you deserved to go to prison." Her laughter rippled through her and latched onto SJ.

"I was so adamant that prison was the next step." He grew quieter as he continued, "But that wasn't why I was crying."

"No, you were crying because you said you knew better. You were crying because you were told to do something, but you didn't." She let go of his hand only to place hers on the left side of his face. "You were crying because you thought I wouldn't love you anymore."

"Yes. But, Mom, what I didn't tell about that day was Who I disobeyed." She cocked her head and looked into her son's eyes for answers. "Mom," he choked on a sob before he whispered, "I disobeyed the Lord." She let go of his hand and held him. This time, he encircled his arms around her and clung to her while he cried.

After taking a moment to breathe deeply, he added, "He encouraged me to sign up for the talent show. He wanted me to sing. But I didn't want to." He looked away as he explained, "I was so scared. And I didn't understand why He would ask me to do something like that, something so not *me*. I know now that He doesn't ask us to do things we are not capable of and that He does ask us to obey Him and to trust Him. No matter what." Tears came to her eyes as she looked at her son, at the man of God he had become. "So, Mom, I need you to trust me when I tell you what I came here to tell you." She stood up straighter. "But I need you to trust Him more."

After a moment of hesitation, she replied, "Oh, baby, you know that I trust Him."

"I know, Mom. But let's go get Dad so I can tell you both at the same time." If they were having any other conversation, she would have teased him for being so dramatic, for building up the suspense. He always had been earnest. But she had never seen it manifest like this before.

"Hi, Dad!" He knocked on the door as he poked his head around to see his dad sitting in his soft blue recliner reading a book, something by Loui Lamoure. It wasn't until SJ stood right in front of him that Jonathan looked up.

"SJ! It is great to see you, son! What brings you by?" He closed the book, but not before he made sure to firmly secure the book mark in its rightful place. Standing up, he wrapped his arms around SJ. "How's my girl?"

"Anja is doing really well, Dad. She wanted to stop by today, but she had a wedding emergency. I need to talk to you and mom."

"All right, son! Let's talk." He smiled and gestured for SJ to go out of the room first. So SJ headed for the dining room table. He didn't see his father lean over and kiss his mom as he wrapped his arms around her waist before they followed his lead.

Sitting down at the stained oak table with the sunshine and sky blue runner, he gestured for them to sit next to him.

"Uh…there is something I need to tell you." He didn't want to acknowledge that he saw his mom crying. Not loudly. Not obviously. But the tears were there. Even if they weren't yet falling. He looked down at his hands as his fingers rubbed against each other. "I'm joining the marine corps."

He waited for a laugh, for a smile, for a scream, a shout, anything. But nothing came. Not from her. "Well, son. If that is what you want. But what about Anja?"

"Oh, you don't have to worry about Anja. She can take care of herself. And—"

"I know she can, son. But that does not mean that she should have to." He knew his father was right. But there was a plan. He knew it. Even if he couldn't see it.

He let the Spirit take over. "You are right. But God has a plan for me, and He wants me to go serve in the marine corps. All of it has been arranged. I head out in two weeks." After he graduated from boot camp, he would marry the woman of his dreams...and pray he would then be stationed in San Diego. Anywhere to be as close to her as possible.

"That...that isn't a lot of time."

"Uh... I know. I really do. This seems like a blur, but He has been preparing me for a while."

"How, son? You were about to graduate with a Bachelor's in ag business to start your own business with Anja. And now you are going to leave your job, your girl, your parents...your whole life?" He could have mentioned that the marines would help him finish school and get his degree, but that didn't matter right now. Not as much as her.

"Uh...you are missing one thing." His dad just furrowed his eyebrows, so he explained, hoping to change the subject, "She is not just my girl, Dad." Still, Jonathan just shook his head. "She is my fiancé." There was no special moment, though. It dispersed before it even arrived when his mother silently scooted her chair back and walked out the sliding glass door just before the fire alarm went off.

4

The Aftermath

Only four more feet. At least that's what he hoped for as trees whipped past him. It didn't matter that his ankle was screaming as he pushed harder, ran faster. It didn't matter that his team was several feet behind him. It didn't matter that the enemy could attack him at any second, that he could drop at any second without a moment more to live. Because she was right there. And he had to get to her.

So he pushed harder through the trees, the brush, the barricades that tried to prevent him from getting to her. He prayed she knew that *nothing* would stop him from reaching her. One more pounding step after another, forward with the force and power of a lion, just like his men called him. And he would not fail his men, his God, and especially not his love. As the forest opened up, he could see Anja, in a cage, in the middle of a grassy field full of lilac. He stopped for less than a split second to take in the scope of potential threats. The field was bordered by the thickest forest he had ever endured in this part of the world. Passing his inspection, he took off. One step closer to freedom. One step closer to peace. One step closer to her.

After stumbling forward from the momentum that fueled his progression, the cage with his wife in it became nothing more than debris and ash. He refused to think about how her body, her beautiful body, no longer had silky, smooth hair that he once ran his fingers through as he listened to her talk about random things that came to her mind. She no longer had lively ocean eyes that he would dive into every time he saw them, especially when he woke up to them awakening his soul. She no longer had fair, soft skin that he would touch as he cupped her face in his hands or as he ran his fingers along her arm in an effort to take away her stress. She didn't exist. Not anymore.

"*No!*" his plea was louder than he thought possible and filled with more sorrow than he ever wanted to endure. He collapsed onto his knees in the field, ignoring the purple flowers and the green grass, and clutched at his heart. *Thump-thump.* His brain willed it to keep beating. *Thump.* Until it didn't any longer.

"*No...*" A hand covered his mouth with enough force to silence him. The hand smelled like dirt, but not just any dirt; this was dirt mixed with residue gun powder and sweat, and it all came back. He was fighting overseas.

He must have fallen asleep because last time he checked, he was talking to Lance Corporal Phillipe Alexander, his best friend on the team. He looked up, and as he would have guessed, it was Phillipe who had his hand over his mouth.

Several minutes passed. Phillipe remained on top of SJ with his hand securely over his mouth. Both were breathing hard. The images were still playing on a loop in his mind as SJ fought to bring himself back to reality, while Phillipe could only wish the enemy had not heard SJ's cry.

Once the "all clear" was given by Sergeant Nathan Bates, Phillipe pushed off SJ to resume a standing position as he shook his head.

"That was close, man. Too close." All SJ could utter was a humble apology. Phillipe saw that SJ's chest still rose and fell too rapidly, so he knelt beside him. "You all right, man?"

"I will be."

With eyebrows angled and a hand extended, Phillipe pressed, "You sure? I mean, I know war is not ideal, but the look on your face"—he pulled SJ up to a standing position—"is not about the war. It's much more than that." It was silent for a few beats as Phillipe gave SJ the opportunity to talk. But that would have to be put on hold: Bates was on his way over. Everyone knew it because they heard what sounded like a bull approaching.

"*Lion!* What was that? You could have gotten us all killed!" By this time, both men faced the man that was in charge.

"Sorry, sir." He placed his hand where it was trained to be every time an authority figure approached him.

"Don't be sorry, Corporal! Be safe!" It must have really been safe, since Bates was not making any effort to be quiet.

"I know, sir. It won't happen again," he tried to mutter it with as much strength as he could, but he knew it wasn't his best.

"I know, Lion." He turned around to see his team and ordered, "Back to your post!" Before he left to return to his station at the north end of their camp, Bates whispered, "You okay?" to which SJ gave him a shaky thumbs up.

After Bates was out of earshot, Phillipe turned to SJ. "It was Anja, wasn't it?" His voice was lower, but there was no mistaking what he said.

"Yeah," that is all SJ could say in return. He didn't overlook that Phillipe didn't miss a beat, that he knew SJ so well that he could pinpoint the cause of his real fear. When he got a second, he would tell Phillipe, even thank him. But he needed a few moments to breathe.

Dear Heavenly Father, please. Please protect her. I know that I am not there to keep her safe, but I am here trying to do so. You needed me here, so I am here. But please. Please be with her always. Never leave her.

Son, I have never left her. And I will never leave you.

I know. I know, but, Father, that dream was too much. I mean, I can't go through that again. I need You. A lot. Especially now. Please give me the strength to keep going. And please, please let me return to her.

Be still, son, and know that I am your God.

Okay, Lord. We will do it Your way. Every time. I just need Your help to see Your hand in my life. But more importantly, to see Your hand in her life. In the name of Jesus Christ, amen.

"What happened?" Phillipe deserved to know.

SJ found the mossy fallen log that he had used as a pillow and leaned up against it, raising his knees to chin level and draping his arms on his knees as his fingers played with a chunk of moss. Phillipe joined him on the ground. SJ took a deep breath, trying to hide the way his body shuddered under the uniform.

"I lost her." He shook his head in an attempt to dispel the images from his mind. "I lost her, man." He couldn't bring himself to look Phillipe in the eyes. He couldn't let Phillipe see his tears. So he stared straight ahead. The rays of the sun barely showed above the dense forest that surrounded them, but it was a sight for sore eyes.

"Aw, man. You are full of surprises." SJ sucked in what tears he could before turning to face Phillipe.

"What do you mean?"

"Look around you! We are at war in the middle of a forest in unknown territory fighting for our lives, and you are here worrying about your wife, who is probably at home cooking dinner for your parents right now." He used gestures with his arms to further emphasize his disbelief.

"What can I say, man?"

"How about something along the lines of 'I'm crazy'?" Phillipe let out a chuckle, still amazed.

"Oh, that I am, man," he paused before he repeated, "that I am." This time, each word seemed to have more weight. After a few more moments, he elaborated, "I'm crazy in love." Both of them quietly lost it as SJ's cheesy grin contributed to the lightheartedness of the moment.

Phillipe sat straighter and friendly slapped SJ on the back. "So, what is the secret souvenir you keep in your pocket?" Phillipe gestured in the direction of SJ's left chest pocket. SJ let out a chuckle. Of course, Phillipe noticed.

"It's a gift from my parents." Instead of a witty remark or a joke, Phillipe just looked at SJ, waiting. "When I was born, they gave me a Winnie the Pooh. But I loved it so much that the fabric wore out, and all of the beans fell out." He let himself laugh. "It was bad, man. But instead of just throwing it away"—a tear found its way to his chin—"my mom put stuffing in it and sewed it up for me." He looked down into his lap. "I have kept him with me every day since I left." It was a reminder that his mom loved him. No matter what.

Phillipe leaned on his right arm as he lifted his body so he could reach into his left back pocket. It was a piece of paper. Once upon a time, it was white, and whole. "This was the very first note my mom ever wrote to me. I found it in my lunch box. Back then, I believed that if I held onto the note, she would stay with me always. Even if she was sick."

"How is she now?" It was barely audible, but no one else needed to hear it.

"She died, man. The cancer got her. But that doesn't mean she is gone. Now I keep it as a reminder of what I couldn't believe then: she never really left. And she never will." Silence settled. "All right, man! I have to know!" Phillipe wrung his hands together, preparing himself for what he hoped would come. "What happened after you two hugged in the romantic location of Little Caesars?"

Sensing what Phillipe was trying to do, he played along and closed his eyes. "Well, neither of us wanted to let go, but we did, so we could order some pizza. I mean, we both went there for pizza, so I bought us pizza." His eyes danced as it always does when he thinks of Anja. "It took another fifteen minutes of discussing what type of pizza to get. She insisted on getting pepperoni on flat crust, but I wanted the traditional crust. We laid out the pros and cons of each, and then we just got one of each. I tried the flat crust, but traditional is still way better. When you meet her though, don't tell her I said that. We still have very different opinions about it. Then I asked her where she wanted to eat it, and she didn't have a preference. I chose to go back to my apartment since I had just cleaned it that day." Phillipe continued to listen. "We just ate pizza and talked. She ate almost half of her pizza, and I ate half of mine." He chuckled before adding, "But her appetite impressed me. She loves food, just like me, man."

"Aw, don't go all fairytale on me."

SJ pushed him and then remarked, "That wasn't even that bad."

"It was about to be." Both of them laughed quietly with each other, and SJ knew Phillipe was right.

"Anyway, we talked really late into the evening. But that's it. We just talked. I felt like we were catching up on the years we had missed." Even if Phillipe wasn't sure about them knowing each other before, he enjoyed their story. It gave him hope, hope for a future with a family, certainly not soon, but eventually. "After that—"

A gunshot whistled just above their heads.

5

The Letter

The clock reads five o'clock in the evening as she sits at her desk, the desk that SJ bought her for her birthday last year. She is a writer like me. If you ask her, though, she calls herself a journalist. But she writes more for herself and her future family. Her desk is wooden with a drawer that shadows a shelf to the right of where her chair fits. One of the two decorations on her desk includes a picture of Jesus Christ holding a staff and looking over Jerusalem. They got it as a wedding gift from his parents.

And there is the other picture. She played with that thick blonde hair on his head. She tenderly grazed her lips on that cheek. She grasped that hand and held it against her chest. She rested her head on that lap when she wanted him to play with her hair.

In the picture, he is standing right behind her with his hands on the rope that is holding up the swing. She is sitting on the swing with her hands stretched behind her and around his waist. Her favorite part is his face. He is looking down at her in a way that leaves no room for confusion or doubt. He has that look, that look that people talk about when they just know that two people are in love.

It wasn't planned, wasn't posed for. His mom had stopped by for a surprise dinner. When she couldn't find them inside, she knew where to find them. Anja didn't used to like the idea of them living in her parents' house once they were newly married. It was just a reminder of her past, her wrongs, her betrayal. But it is what she wanted. It was what she had left of her past, at least the good parts of it. Her mother-in-law captured the moment when she stepped off the back porch. Anja is grateful she did.

She clings to that moment. It was when everything was normal. They had just moved the last load of their stuff to the house in southern California; they wanted it all moved while he could help her. She had a diamond ring on her finger. Her mother-in-law was on board. No, she was more than on board. Rebecca had waited for SJ to ask Anja for what felt like years. So had Anja. Her father-in-law had walked up behind his wife just after she took the picture, wrapped his arms around her, knocked the phone out of her hand, leaned down, and kissed her cheek. She turned to face him, and they kissed again. This time, a little longer. Anja didn't see any of it. She was too caught up in the man that looked at her the way she had only dreamed about, with those eyes that melted her heart no matter how many times she had seen them.

Pen in hand, she started to write. This time, though, she wants her writing to leave the office.

To my love,

Well, things are going here at home. Just going. I would even say things are okay. Just okay. I know that we can FaceTime, but it isn't the same, and I know that we agreed to let you go serve, but I didn't realize I would be letting you go for so long. I feel like I am losing you, and it kills me. We used to tell each other everything, but now I don't even know where you are. I cannot even look at a map. Not that I would want to anyway; it's just a reminder that you are somewhere in that vast expanse of the unknown. Somewhere I can't hear your voice. Somewhere I can't smell your old spice cologne. Somewhere I can't kiss your lips. Somewhere I can't hold you. Somewhere I can't see your eyes.

Did I ever tell you that your eyes gave you away? When we first met, I was only looking down as you held the door open because I had seen your eyes just prior. I knew I had found you. I was smiling, but it wasn't my full smile. I'm sure you know that. It was the I'm-holding-back-because-I-have-finally-found-him smile. I prayed about you every day. I still do. But back then, it was to find you. That He would lead me to you. And guess what?

I found you! And just for the record, I win! I mean, I found you before you found me. So, I win. I think I deserve a win every now and then. Right?

So…here's the thing, love. I have got to say that I was crying a lot, but not right now. I feel better. Like you are here with me and I am just talking to you: how it used to be.

I miss those days. When you were here with me every day. Do you? I think about the past every day. I know I shouldn't. It probably isn't very healthy for me. But I can't help it. I am trying to be strong. But I'm not always. Is that okay?

Do you still love me? Sorry, I think I know that answer. I just need to be reminded, I guess.

But don't worry, I will keep talking and you can listen! Deal?

I was recently thinking about your mother. I saw her the other day. I actually see her often. We have agreed that we need each other more than we may acknowledge. She talks about you a lot. But she never mentions the war. That topic is off limits. And the fact that you are gone. She walks away if it is brought up. But I don't do it that often. (It isn't my favorite topic either.) It has been good talking to her. I know that I definitely talk more, but she is starting to open up more to me. I know she loves me and that she has been our number one fan this whole time. But ever since you left, she has gotten quieter. Actually, I think it started when you told her. Sorry, I'm not blaming you. I just want you to know. I have been praying for her, though. Will you pray with me? And your dad is doing well! As I am sure you know, he writes to you often. They both miss you. We all do.

And now, on to other things that are on my mind. (Don't worry…there is more!) Do you remember the first night we met? And the next several months? We were together every single day. I was so scared I would want my space. You know how much I like my personal space, time to myself, all of that greatness. Wait, do you? Love, do you know that about me? Anyway, on with the story! It was the opposite, though; I wanted more time with you. I wanted more of you. Oh, and before you bring it up, I am not counting my weekend trip to central California. I know I wasn't with you for three days, but it went so quickly it doesn't even count.

So thank you for giving me all of you. Even if you are miles and miles away from me, in more than one way, thank you. I am so grateful to the Lord for you. Did you know that I thank Him every day? Every morning and even throughout the day, I make sure He knows how grateful I am for you. For April 22. For life before this. Mostly for you being a part of me. I knew He would answer my prayers to find you, but I didn't think it would be on my way to get pizza at Little Caesars. But in case I haven't mentioned this before, thank you for wanting pizza the evening of April 22.

Well, I haven't started dinner yet, but I probably should. I was thinking of making Grandma's breaded chicken: our first meal together. I would save some for you, but please don't be mad if it is all gone before tomorrow.

How about I mix the breading and you cut the chicken? I haven't always been careful with knives, or so you say.

Don't worry, love. I know you will respond as soon as you can. And I look forward to it. See you soon.

No matter what,
Anja

She couldn't bring herself to tell him about her new realization. The one that started to blossom the moment he told her his new path. The one that grew little by little more and more each day. The one that, if she let it, would take her down sooner rather than later. And yet, it was the one she knew to be true. Without a doubt. Because no matter what prayers they offered, no matter what promises they made to each other, the man she knew and loved would not be the one to return.

6

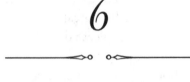

The Gift

"Hello, darling!" Rebecca walked up to her as she walked in the front door. In less than six seconds Anja had her shoes off.

"Hello, Mama." Rebecca knew Anja didn't want to call her "Mommy." And she understood. Only one person had been her mommy; there was no changing that.

They held each other for several minutes. Both of them knew what it was like to have him gone, what it was like to pray every day for his safe return, what it was like to try to trust God, but to also wonder why. Jonathan walked into the entryway and wrapped his arms around both of them.

After he let go, he clapped his hands as if to dispel the sadness. "Well, time for dinner!" The women released each other just as Jonathan wrapped his arms around his girls and led them toward the kitchen. Before they stepped into it, he asked Anja to close her eyes; she hadn't seen the new kitchen yet. Adjusting so he could guide her by her shoulders, Jonathan walked behind her. The fire had destroyed most of the kitchen, but they embraced it as a blessing. I mean, the kitchen was really old. (You don't need to know how old.)

"Okay, now you can look!" He squeezed her shoulders. She opened her eyes to see a new kitchen with stainless steel appliances. The stovetop revealed five burners, each with a corresponding display. The fridge had two doors instead of one, and the shell glimmered. She knew it wouldn't stay that clean for long, but she would admire it for now. They even got a new sink. Well, two sinks. It was a double sink, one of which was at least half a foot deep.

A smile grew on her face.

Dear Heavenly Father, thank You for blessing them. Thank You for blessing my in-laws, for keeping them safe, for helping them to rebuild. And thank You for the new kitchen. I know that Rebecca and Johnny love it. In the name of Jesus Christ, amen.

"It is beautiful!" She turned to face them. They were holding hands and smiling at her. She knew they weren't smiling because of their new kitchen. Although, both of them would enjoy it; they loved to cook. In fact, they took turns throughout the week. Anja and SJ had done that too. He learned to cook from his parents, so while he is away, she has been trying to perfect her cooking skills. That way, when he comes home, she will win the cooking contests they have. Lucky for her, she gets to learn from the best!

They were smiling because she was there. Together. As much as they could be, at least.

Distracted by the new appliances, Anja did not notice until she took a deep breath that they had also cooked dinner—her grandma's breaded chicken recipe. There was no mistaking it.

After another hug, they all sat down at the table. She served herself a plate of a breaded chicken breast, buttered vegetables, and mashed potatoes. She sprinkled some salt and pepper on her potatoes and was ready to eat. After a prayer on the food, they dug in. She proceeded to clean the glass pan they had used to cook the chicken before the plate was even clear. You see, there is almost nothing better than toasted olive oil and bread crumbs. Not exactly healthy, but she made sure to treat herself every once in a while.

"Thank you so much. It was delicious!"

"Not as good as your grandmother made it, I am sure, but I tried."

She couldn't help but notice one tear fell as she replied, "Don't worry, Mama. It was amazing."

"Well, your father helped too." He gently slammed his fist on the table.

"It's not every day I get permission to get my hands dirty in the kitchen. I was a master of rolling the chicken in the bread crumbs and oil, if I do say so myself." He puffed his chest out just a little, like SJ does.

"Well, I give you my official stamp of approval to cook this meal anytime you want and every time you want!"

"That just means you will have to come over more often." All of them smiled, especially Anja.

"Now *that* I will most certainly do." She took an extra moment to look at them. She could see SJ in them—Rebecca's heart, Johnny's endurance. There was no mistaking it.

"So, darling, how is work?" Mama was always the one to ask her about work. Papa just wanted to know how she was doing. But they didn't always get that far into the conversation.

"It is going well. There have been a lot of weddings, even in January, so that keeps me pretty busy." She took a deep breath. "But I love it!"

"And you are so good at it, I am sure. If I was getting married, I would ask you to plan my wedding, but I'm already hitched." They joined in a chorus of laughter as they all recalled their story. Johnny had asked Rebecca in the car on their way to visit his family if she wanted to get hitched. I know he will never live that down, as do they.

"So how is work for you two?" Rebecca is a substitute teacher and Johnny works on a dairy.

"Good! I substituted in a classroom today, and the kids and I worked really well together. It was an answer to my prayers. I don't usually like subbing at that school, but today may have changed my mind. At least for that class. They are so darling!"

"I love hearing when you have good days in the classroom! The Lord is so good at answering prayers."

It got quiet for a moment, and then Papa chimed in, "The cows are doing well! But they miss you." Anja laughed because she actually missed them too. She and SJ used to spend quality time on the dairy just talking to the cows. He always used to say that they all have unique personalities, but she wouldn't believe it until she saw it for herself. It was the one time she gave him credit for being right. She made a note to visit the dairy soon. It would be an opportunity to surprise Johnny!

"It is good to know they have not forgotten me." She giggled. "Did I ever tell you that my first word was 'moo'? I don't even know why, but that was the first word I ever spoke."

"It was not!" Mama's mouth gaped open. "That was SJ's first word!" She put her hand to her chin and looked up as if looking for clarification. "He spoke that one word for days before he said anything else. The next word he ever spoke was 'papa.' He took a few more weeks to say 'mama,' but I think he did it on purpose."

"Oh, I know he did."

"Speaking of SJ, he got you something." Mama jumped out of her seat and practically skipped out of the room as she disappeared down the hall. Papa's eyes just glimmered with mischief, and she knew something was up the second she heard it.

She turned to see him—Jake. She and SJ had already picked out a name for the dog they would get one day. And there he was. Sliding down the hall. She wondered if they should have named him Butterball. That's what he looked like, after all. A buttery yellow with a hint of brown. But his nose was black and looked like that of a German shepherd while the top of his paws was white. Those floppy ears just about undid her, but she had lost control anyway. She met him halfway as he slid right into her bent knees.

"Oh, Jakie. You weren't supposed to do that." She laughed some more as she picked him up, feeling Australian shepherd fur and placing his nose in front of her face. "Hi, Jakie! Hi, handsome boy!" She covered her mouth and looked at her parents. "Don't tell SJ that I called our dog handsome." They ran their fingers across their lips and threw away the key almost at the same time. This was the most they had smiled in a while. She walked over to them, and they all embraced, while avoiding crushing the butterball. As she stepped back, they all saw her tears, but no one said anything.

"His kennel and bed are in the room, and we bought some food to help you start your new life with that adorable bundle of fur."

Without thinking about it, she started swaying back and forth and lightly bouncing. She didn't notice it until Mama pointed it out. And it's okay. Jake fell asleep in his mom's arms, just as she had dreamed about when she and SJ first started talking about getting a dog. It was something else they did together, something else they had planned together—a future they dreamed about together. Yet, it was only her. But there was no time to think about that now.

After a lot of petting and cooing, Anja decided to call it a night. Papa loaded the bed, kennel, and food into her 1990 Blazer while the women shared hugs. He gave Anja a hug just before she situated the sleeping Jake on the passenger seat and got into the truck to drive home for the night.

"Good night, darling! See you soon!" Mama and Papa waved as she drove out of the driveway, headed home. Well, to what used to be home. Now with Jake, it can start to feel like home again. And no, Jake isn't SJ, but, like SJ, Jake is an extension of God's love for her—a home she has yet to discover.

7

The Test

"Why would he do that, Johnny? Why would he send me seven letters this time? He knows it's my favorite number."

"Exactly, sweetheart. That's why. He knows that, and he wants to remind you." He walked up to her and started to scratch her back as she leaned over the kitchen table clutching a letter in her fingers.

"But he doesn't get to do that. He doesn't get to..." She shoved all of the letters off the table as she plopped into the chair. Sobbing, she repeated, "He doesn't get to do that. To remind me of what he knows. What he left. He doesn't get to do that." Johnny pulled the nearest chair closer to him and settled on her left.

"Sweetheart, you and I know he is obeying the Lord. He is doing what he is supposed to be doing."

"How can you say that?" She didn't mean to scream. But it was more a scream of frustration. She doesn't like not being in control. She hasn't ever really liked it. It had been two years. He hadn't been back in two years. After he and Anja got married, he left and hasn't come back. Jake is already one. And SJ hasn't seen any of it. He hasn't even sent anything in months. Until today: his birthday.

Johnny grabbed her hand and led her to their bedroom. He let go and sat down on the end of the bed. He could see the tears in her eyes, feel her pain, so he waited.

And then she walked up to the bed and sat down in front of him. She could feel him breathing against her neck and breathed deeply as he wrapped his arms around her waist. And then he squeezed. They didn't need to talk about it right now. After all, they had been for two years.

It seemed to be a different reaction every time, but every once in a while, everything she felt came out in anger. He tried to help her, to get her to talk so that she didn't bottle everything up inside. But after twenty-one years of trying, they were still working on it. And that's okay. He would always be there to hold her, especially when she cried.

Sometimes they cried together. Only Rebecca was allowed to see all of him. It has been that way for as long as they have known each other. And he had no doubt it would be that way for eternity.

"You are my sunshine, my Becky sunshine. You make me happy when skies are gray. You'll never know, boo, how much I love you. Please don't take my sunshine away." It was her song. The first song he ever sang for her. He didn't like to brag, but he certainly has a voice of gold, at least Rebecca and I think so. His singing voice is what helps her fall asleep when she wakes up from nightmares about marines knocking on her door to tell her that her son would never come home. The marine in charge of his team and that of other teams, a Master Sergeant Jay Beck, had informed them about that procedure, just in case. She wished they never would have told her. Sometimes not knowing is better.

He sang that verse over and over as he held onto her for almost an hour. After a while, though, he let his head rest on her shoulder, where he silently shed tears. He understood the pain, the nightmares, the fear, the faith, the trust, the hope. All of it. He tried so hard to be strong for her. But sometimes he had to let himself feel, to let go. And he only did it with her, and Him.

Father in heaven, I won't ask why. I am trying to trust that You know why. Why You sent him away. Why he is celebrating his birthday all alone. But please, continue to protect him. Continue to let him know that he is so loved. In the name of Jesus Christ, amen.

Hours later, he woke up. But she wasn't there. He found her at the kitchen table crying as her shaking hands held a letter with his handwriting. She had picked up the letters. Four were turned over to her right, the fifth one in her hand.

"Sweetheart…" He didn't know what to say. He sat on her right and slid the letter out from the bottom of the stack. Each letter was free of creases, since he fit them all in the manila envelope, but Becky's tears left ink smudges. He skimmed the letter until something caught his eye at the bottom.

> So, I had a nightmare the other day. But I don't want to go into detail. Instead, let me tell you about what happened after it. I talked to my new best friend, Phillipe Alexander. Don't get me wrong, Anja is my best friend for eternity. We call each other BFFEs. Did you know that? Anyway, he and I have become best buds. He saved my life, actually. This is not to scare or worry you, but to let you know something I should have told you a long time ago. Ever since I was born, I have felt so loved, so cherished. I don't think I ever took the time to thank you. Both of you. And, Mama, I am sorry. I know this is hard, for all of us, but thank you for loving me anyway. Papa, thank you for always having my back. Both of you taught me what it is like to be loved and to love. Now I get to share that love with my teammates. The love of brothers, but more importantly, the love of God. The love I share with Anja. It means a lot to me what I have been able to do here. While it is still hard, I take comfort in knowing that He is in control. I wouldn't want it any other way.
>
> All my love,
> SJ

More tears fell as Johnny realized that God really was there, that He had always been there, and He always would be. God loves SJ more than anyone ever would, more than anyone ever could. It was just a matter of letting go.

8

The Man

Phillipe was trying to tell him something, but his hand motions were a blur. Was he holding up eight fingers? Or no fingers? The noise from the gunshots weren't helping. He shook his head. It was time to focus. Phillipe and he had made up their own hand signals; each motion meant something different. They even shared it with the team so no words had to be uttered while in tense, life-threatening situations. Like this one.

It looked like Phillipe was making half a heart with his left hand, which only meant one thing. SJ needed to complete it. Just in case. So he did. Raising his right hand, he completed the heart and knew he would forever be grateful for Phillipe, for his team, for his life. But today was not the day to reflect. Today was the day to fight. He flipped over onto his stomach, ears still ringing, and he fired. Bullet after bullet shot out of the M16 A4 rifle as he aimed it at the targets. The real targets. The targets that breathed, just like him. The targets that were fighting, just like him. The targets that had killed other people, just like him.

Still more bullets lunged themselves from the figures that stood surrounding him and his team. It was strange, though, because they blended in with their surroundings. Not just because of the leaves draping their figures and the dark soil smudged on their faces. It was their eyes. Or lack thereof. There was no soul.

It was like looking at a dead body. As he fired, he shot dead men, he shot dead sons, he shot death. Their bodies were firing guns right back at SJ and his team, but despite the movement, it was from men and boys whose lives were already taken, whose lives were gone, even before the bullets hit them repeatedly in the chest and before the bullets tore through their flesh, puncturing lungs, plugging hearts, and rupturing brains.

But it wasn't just the enemy who had figures going down. He knew it when he heard their cry. The voices of Sergeant Bates and Lance Corporal Phillipe Alexander blended together as he watched Private First Class Oliver Talbert drop. His anguish joined the chorus. Not because the bullet ruptured the popliteal artery in Talbert's left thigh.

It was because SJ knew. There was too much burgundy streaming down Talbert's pants and collecting in a pool at his feet. In a matter of minutes, he would take his last breath, that no matter what he wanted, no matter how hard he tried, there would be nothing that would let him take another breath. Not even one.

"Stew!" he heard Phillipe call out Talbert's nickname—the nickname he acquired after he puked up a bowl of stew during one of their first drills together. It was the day they became a team, one bound by more than just the blood, sweat, and sleepless nights they shared.

SJ couldn't move. He watched as Phillipe crept lower, moving one long, slow, crouched step at a time closer to Stew, his brother. But SJ had to stay there.

Private Damian Munoz stood at his one o'clock, hiding his strong, yet thin body behind a palm tree while shooting at the enemy as they relentlessly tried to take all of them out. SJ could feel Private Zaryn Day's intense, blue gaze as he lied on his stomach at his three o'clock and used a rock as his perch, firing his A4 rifle like his life depended on it. Lance Corporal Forest Wheeler's ears hid beneath his camouflage helmet as he squatted at SJ's four o'clock behind the trunk of a tree, aiming for the enemy's vulnerabilities. Private First Class Connor Deeks, who had the steadiest hands of anyone SJ had ever met, took aim at his six o'clock from behind a cluster of trees, covering SJ's back. SJ, along with every member of his team, heard the orders Sergeant Nathan Bates was barking from SJ's eight o'clock with an urgency to rid them of their oppressors. Lance Corporal Phillipe Alexander with skin almost as dark as their surroundings continued to step backward at his ten o'clock, inching closer to Private First Class Oliver Talbert, whose round face was hidden beneath a mirror of tears.

All he could think about was Talbert, why he was really weeping. It wasn't the pain. It was because he would never get to hold his wife in his arms as they watch their son sleep, hear his son laugh as he runs around the kitchen wearing the lid of a pot as his hat, see his wife bite her lip when she knows she is right, taste his three-year-old son's snot as he sneezes while Talbert holds him above his face and spins him around just after he walks through the front door, smell his wife's nail polish remover, indicating that she gave up on it only moments after putting it on.

It felt like hours as SJ remained locked in place, refusing to move for the sake of the safety and well-being of his team. Or most of them.

By the time he reached Talbert, he was gone.

Silence. No tears or shouts could bring him back. Yes, it was part of the job. But no, it wasn't supposed to happen. No, it wasn't easy. No, it wasn't fair. And no, it wasn't time. It never was.

The flag that he had grown to loathe hugged the casket. Don't get me wrong, he loved it, always had and always will. But it just reminded him of everything he had lost. He still respected it, what it stood for, who it longed to protect. But the red stripes also included the blood of Private First Class Oliver Talbert. The white stripes flaunted the loss of their minds, the disappearance of morality and purity that comes with war. The white stars represented how many pieces of their souls were ripped away one shot at a time. The blue rectangle foreshadowed the casket that each one of them would find themselves in one way or another. If they were lucky, the blue sky was the last thing they saw.

He and his brothers hauled his cherry wood casket toward the brace that awaited it. He and Lance Corporal Phillipe Alexander took the front two handles with Private Munoz, Private Day, Lance Corporal Wheeler, and Private Deeks marching behind them. Sergeant Bates took the lead, just like he always did.

Eyes forward. Ears alert. Mouths straight. Fists clenched. Based on appearances, they were there to do a job all the way up to a hole that resembled what they lived in, as needed. No one saw the pain underneath. It was an ache that never truly goes away, an ache for one more breath, one more chance that never comes.

9

The Secret

There he was. Nine drafts later. How was he supposed to tell her that he had been back in the continental United States, but they didn't see each other? Not that she even knew he was so close. He had wanted to tell her but couldn't.

The camp was all set up. Tents dotted the dry landscape with a variety of tables, equipment, including guns, and slop some call food. It was the best they could do. They were always on the go. But not today.

He didn't dare venture far, but it was enough for him to be alone, especially now. So, there he was on his ninth draft. Crumples of paper lay beneath and next to his outstretched legs. He placed the paper on the cookie sheet while the pen shook in his right hand. He so badly wanted to see her face, but he couldn't bring himself to call her; he didn't know how to tell her what was going on, what he was going through. Besides, they agreed on sending each other letters. It helped them to keep that tradition alive.

Dear Father in heaven, I know You are there, but it doesn't always seem like it. I know I haven't talked to You that much recently. I just felt like I didn't have time. And there may have been some anger in there too. But I am sorry. I do have time. He shook his head. *I always do. I just don't think I can handle all of this. I know You think I can. But losing Talbert was hard, Lord. Too hard. At least he is with You.* He took a deep breath.

He is with You, which is better than being here. He dropped the pen, grabbed a handful of the hottest dirt he had ever touched, and threw it to the side. *But I am where You need me to be. I believe that.* He let a tear fall down his cheek. *No regrets. I just can't get that image out of my head. There was more blood than I have ever seen. And I just couldn't help but picture...* Another tear fell. And then another. There was no stopping it. *Her. Father, what if it was her?* A few more sobs escaped from his heart as his lips quivered.

I know she isn't here. I know she is safe in Your hands, but a part of me wants her here just so that I can hold her, so I can tell her that I am okay, that I am safe, that I trust You. I know she knows all of that. Or I hope she does. Father...

You want her.

Another sob escaped as he tried to catch his breath. *Yes. I am not trying to demote You. You know that. But she is my life. My everything. I love her. With all of me. I love You more, but, Father, a love like ours doesn't come around every day.* He let out a brief laugh. *Thanks to You, Your plans, Your timing.* He wiped his face with one swipe of his arm. *Well, I need to ask for Your help. I need You always. I need You to show me why I am here. I went along with Your plan, but it is harder than I thought, and honestly, I don't see what I am doing here. I feel like I am just getting deeper and deeper into a hole that I won't be able to escape from. One that takes me away from my parents, from Anja, from You. Because I just don't see Your plan. And it is really hard to see You.* He allowed a brief chuckle to escape. *Sorry. I know that is a lot. Will You please give me the words to tell her what happened, to tell her how I feel? And please let her know that I still love her. Please, please keep her safe.*

Trust Me, SJ. I know what is best for you, when it is best for you, and how it is best for you. I love you, My son.

Father, thank You. I love You too. He nodded. *You are the author of my life and her life. Thank You. In the name of Jesus Christ, amen.*

He grabbed the pen from his lap and held it, waiting, hoping, praying. Well, at least he knew where to start. Pulling out the dusty, slightly torn letter from his pants pocket, he placed it on his heart. It brushed his lips as he held it out in front of him. It was the closest he had been to her since he left. After he graduated boot camp, he was stationed in San Diego, only half an hour from where they lived. At least they were able to keep her parents' house. It was another answered prayer. He didn't want to uproot her more than he had.

He didn't know how long he would be away, and he really didn't know if he would make it home. Maybe that was what God had called him to do. Maybe death was his path. But there was no time to think about that now. All of it was in His hands. So, he began to write.

Love,

This may not help, but I cannot tell you where I am. I don't know if I ever will be able to tell you. But don't worry about looking at a map, love. I can do that for you. I will look at it and point to where I will be headed soon, where I will hear your laugh, where I will smell your coconut milk shampoo, where I will kiss your lips, where I will hold you and never let go, where I will look into your eyes and never look away. I hope you know I never ever want to leave you. I do believe that God wants me to be here, to serve here, even if I cannot see it. And if this is where He wants me to be, then here I am. You know, love, I want to be His hands, to do His will. Even if that means me being here.

Now, about your eyes. The eyes that gave you away. I was taught to respect the women in my life, to honor them, and to love them. I do so with my mother, as I do with you. But I definitely recognized you first. You may have seen my eyes first, said something first, but my heart knew it before you did. Sorry, love, but I knew with all of me that I had found you. I didn't tell anyone, but I knew it first. So, I win. Sorry again. (Or am I?)

Besides, you win almost all of the time. Except for now. Since I won this time around.

But I cry too. Not in front of the guys, of course, but I do. Just before writing this, I did. Because I want you. All of you. Here with me. Well, not where I am. I wouldn't wish this upon anyone. Ever. But I still trust Him. I always will.

Do you know that I think about you every day? I picture you with me. Sometimes we are on the beaches of San Diego, one of our favorite places, or Little Caesars, where it all began, or even just at home as I wake up to look into your ocean. So, I guess we are both guilty of wanting more, wishing for better. But maybe that isn't bad. Because He wants what is best for us. He loves when we dream. So don't stop, baby. Keep dreaming! Keep hoping! Keep praying! He hears you. And He will blow your mind with blessings. We can't see it now, but they are coming.

Just make sure you don't forget to be grateful for what you have, for what He has given you. Live where you are because it is where He wants you to be, where He needs you to be. And, love, you don't have to be strong 24-7. No one is. That is when we let Him carry us. And He will.

I am sorry that I haven't been in more contact. I could come up with excuses, but there is no time in this life for them. So, I'm sorry.

But, princess, please, please do not ever doubt my love for you. It is deeper than the oceans. I know that sounds cliché, but it's true. You are my breath, my life, my love. I am yours in every way. And I am always willing and want to listen to you. You have always been my thinker.

I saw the change in my mom when I told her. I knew it was coming when I walked into the house. She wasn't prepared for that. It is my fault. I sprung it on her. But I am so glad she still opens up to you. And I get my dad's letters. They help a lot. I can sense my mom is a part of them too. Even if her name is not on them. But I miss her. A lot.

And I'll have you know those three days were the longest days of my life. And I am still so sorry I didn't go with you. I know you didn't want me to, but I felt I should have. To be with you as you faced your past, your loss. But I want you to know that you have come so far. And I am here for you! Now and for eternity!

Did you know that I had a countdown to the day we got married? November 4, 2015, changed my life for eternity. No regrets. Ever. You truly made me the happiest man in the universe that day. I don't know if words can describe how much I love you. How much you mean to me. Love, I am yours. Always.

So, thank you! Even more so for putting up with my bad hair days, for enduring my goofy spells, for loving all of me. No matter what. Thank you for remembering me. I knew I knew you, and you knew you knew me. It was certainly all Him. I am grateful to Him every day as well. He is at the head of our marriage, and I love that. I love that He is there, protecting you, watching over you, loving you, being there for you. He was before I was, and I know He always will be. I am just so grateful that now He and I can both be there for you. The three of us do make quite a team.

I hope you know I am smiling thinking about you. About us. About God. We are never alone, love. I promise.

And I better get some of that chicken when I get home. I'll be counting on it! (No pressure!) And please, please let me take care of cutting the chicken. It is safer for you, me, and the house that way. Oh, and did you get the gift I sent you?

Thank you for making me smile. For making me laugh. For loving me. For all of you.

I hope this doesn't take too long to get there. I will see you soon! Don't you worry! I'm coming home!

No matter what,
SJ

P. S. You deserve to know. I was in San Diego last month for four hours. But it wasn't enough time, since I thought you would be in the central valley to visit your parents. Did you go this year? It was that time of the year. Sorry I wasn't there again. I just didn't want to get our hopes up. But I will see you soon. I promise. Sorry again, love. Please know that I love you with all of me. No matter what.

Well, he told her the only way he knew how. And even then, he hadn't told her all of it. He just didn't know how to deal with it. He didn't even know how he was feeling about it. If he didn't think about, didn't face it, didn't let it linger, then it wouldn't hurt. But he couldn't escape it. So he let more tears flow. No, he didn't know Stew's darkest secret, his greatest fear, his biggest flaw, or even his favorite color. But he did know that Talbert would do anything to save him, to save Phillipe, to save Deeks, to save Munoz, to save Wheeler, to save Day, to save Bates. Even if that meant giving his own life. SJ could no longer hold onto the rising anger. It wasn't Talbert's fault. And SJ couldn't blame him, not even in the least. Because he would do the exact same thing.

10

The Friend

"I can't believe that he wouldn't tell me." Her arms followed through the motion of her shrug by slapping the side of each thigh. "I would have made sure to be there. It is less than an hour away. I mean, much less. I could have made it in ten minutes…" Her voice grew quiet as she realized how inaccurate and unsafe that would be. "I would have dropped everything. I would do anything."

"Does he know that?" Kate sat across from her as she leaned against the arm of the chair, patiently listening.

"What do you mean?"

"Not to doubt you, or your love for him, but does he know what 'anything' means?" Anja's head shot backward. Did he know she would do anything?

"He does. He knows that I wouldn't do anything God wouldn't want me to do, wouldn't need me to do. But that doesn't mean I understand." She reached out and enclosed Kate's hands. "Do you ever feel like you understand His will? I mean, I try, but I don't know if I am successful. I make plans. We make plans and ask for His advice, His input, His approval, and then the Lord just stays silent, or He takes people away from me."

Kate gave an empathetic smile. "Have you ever thought that He does answer your prayers, but the answer is no? He is the best listener. But sometimes, His answers aren't what we are looking for. That doesn't mean He doesn't hear us, that He doesn't love us, that

He wants to cause us harm. He didn't call SJ away to cause you and him pain. But He has a plan, even if it just includes you and him growing closer together because of the distance."

"But we aren't even close. He is thousands of miles away. Maybe. I mean, I don't even know. I just know that he is out there somewhere without me." She swiped a tear that fell before she continued, "But I trust Him. I do. I don't mean to say that and have my words and actions indicate something different. He has tested my patience before, so I have had practice acquiring it, but I thought that was all. I thought He was done testing me that way. I thought I passed."

"How would you describe your love for SJ right now?" Anja lifted her chin so she was looking at Kate.

"Um…present?" Her forehead wrinkled.

"Okay, so what does that mean to you?"

Anja laughed. "Why do I feel like you are serving as my therapist right now?"

Kate's face sobered. "I'm sorry, Anja. I don't mean to come across that way. I can—"

"No, no. You are totally fine. I need this." She squeezed Kate's hands, hoping Kate knew how much it meant to her that she was there listening, even though the church service had concluded over an hour ago. "So, by 'present,' I mean that it is there. Always. I feel it all the time, even if it is just me thinking about him, me reflecting on our past together, me dreaming about what it will be like when he comes home. I feel him all the time."

"Exactly! Even if he isn't with you physically, he is still there. Just like God is. Both of them are there for you. So, maybe God is trying to show you that. No matter what, Anja, He is in control. No matter what, you and SJ are in His hands." Her volume dropped before she hit it home. "No matter what you think or want, He knows best every time."

Anja couldn't pull her eyes away from Kate's. The emeralds that looked back at her seemed familiar, even seemed close, not in a physical way, a way beyond this world.

Without notice, she released Kate's hands and wrapped them around Kate's body. She didn't want to make Kate uncomfortable, but yes, she had met her only a couple hours ago. She was sitting in the south lobby on the armchair, leaning on her elbows and praying. Kate must have seen, for she whispered something to her husband, who nodded. They exchanged a brief kiss, and then he walked outside. Kate took her place in the armchair just across from Anja. After her prayer, Anja looked up to see Kate there. She didn't need introductions, just someone to listen, so she skipped straight to the point, the last two years and six months of it.

After a few moments, Anja loosened her embrace and leaned back. She whipped the bangs out of her face and took a deep breath. Then, grabbing Kate's hands, she stood.

"I just want to thank you so much. Thank you for being there for me, for listening to a stranger." As she looked down, she noticed Kate's beautiful floral dress. Sheer sleeves accentuated her shoulders as pink flowers created a messy, complete pattern on the cream material that cascaded down her body. The pink heels just added to her outfit.

"Oh, honey. It was my pleasure, truly." She smiled. Anja recognized that Kate's outward beauty was accentuated by her beauty from within.

She rubbed her hands together and then folded them in front of her, suddenly becoming more aware. "Sorry, I must be holding you up." She turtled her neck before she apologized again and laughed as she asked, "What is your name?"

"Oh, I am Kate Richardson!" Kate gave Anja another hug. "If you don't have any plans tonight, you are welcome to join my husband and me for dinner tonight."

"Oh, Kate, I don't want to impose." She reached for Kate's hand and squeezed, hoping she knew how much the invitation meant.

"Anja, it isn't an imposition at all. We would love your company." Her smile confirmed her words.

Dear Heavenly Father, thank You for bringing Kate and me into each other's lives.

"My in-laws are out of town tonight, so I would love to join you! Thank you." *Father, please let her know how much it means to me.*

Please bless her for listening to Your Spirit, for not letting me feel alone. In Your Son's name, Jesus Christ, amen.

After putting Kate's address and cell into her phone and jumping into her Blazer, she headed for home and pulled into the driveway only minutes later. Deciding to park outside of the garage, she walked up to the front door and put the key into it. It swung open with ease and invited Jake to come running. Barreling around the corner, he found his way to her and jumped into her arms. Burying her head into his neck, she let the tears come.

She clung to his fur, which she realized only after he winced in pain. Letting go, she wiped the tears that were all too familiar and knelt down beside him.

"I'm sorry, handsome." She laughed as she ignored the fact that she was talking to her puppy. "You just aren't him. Still handsome, but not him." She let out a grunt of frustration. "It isn't supposed to be this way. I worked so hard, tried so hard. But it never goes away." Jake showed off his caramel eyes as he rested his chin on her leg. She saw the apology in his eyes. But it wasn't his fault.

It wasn't his fault that SJ wasn't there. It wasn't his fault that he couldn't replace SJ, that she didn't want him to replace SJ. It wasn't his fault that even with him, she knew someone was missing.

Hey, Daddy? I am sorry for not being grateful like I should be. Jakie is a great addition to this family, but... She didn't want to finish her thought.

He isn't SJ.

No, he isn't. She clenched her teeth and closed her eyes. *And here's the thing. I prayed that this wouldn't happen again, that this would never happen again. But here we are. Once again, I am alone. After my parents died, as You know, I shut You out. Daddy, they left me alone, broken, helpless, and hopeless. I couldn't see a light because there was no light. I had nobody. Not even You. You seemed to abandon me just like they did. But after a year, I found You again.*

He remained quiet, listening.

My first prayers were that I would never feel alone again, that I would never have to feel like my oxygen level was constantly running out. I prayed day and night harder than I ever have before. And it felt so good.

I felt heard, respected, loved. I even found SJ. And then You took him away from me. So, I guess what I am trying to say is what am I doing wrong? I haven't felt alone in so long, but ever since he left, it is worse than when my parents passed away. Daddy, where are You? Why do I feel like I am taking on all of this by myself without any backup?

She waited. Sometimes He answered immediately; sometimes it took longer. The key was to listen.

Lacing her fingers through Jake's fur, she kissed the top of his head before leaning on him. Then, she took just a moment to scream into his fur. Alone.

11

The Irony

"Anja! I'm so happy to see you! Come in!" She tried to force a smile, but there was no need once she saw Kate's arms open wide. They didn't even close the purple door—yes, purple—before they held onto each other in a warm embrace. Then, Kate gestured to the right, down the hall toward what Anja thought was the kitchen.

Before they reached the kitchen, a man reaching six feet and two inches with brunette hair and coffee eyes peaked from behind a wall down the hall and to the left of where they were standing. "You must be Anja." In eleven steps, he reached Anja and shook her hand. "It is nice to meet you." Up closer, she could see what seemed to be a buzz cut. At least once upon a time, it was. But his hair, particularly the caramel locks that rested on top of his head, had grown out a few inches.

"Anja, I can give you a tour of the house before we eat, if you are interested. The pie needs to cook a little while longer before we eat it." Kate lovingly patted Kyle's chest and raised an eyebrow. It was recognizable. She knew that even if Kyle had done something to interrupt the scheduled dinnertime, Kate forgave him. Even more so, she loved him more than she had seconds prior.

"Did I hear we are having pie for dinner?" Anja teased as she went on, "And I would love a tour." Her smile grew as she received welcoming gazes in return. With a skip in her step, Kate linked arms with Anja and turned to the left.

They found themselves in the family room. A wooden desk with a thirty-six-inch screen computer laid in the northeast corner of the room. Just to its right was a blue L-shaped couch that allowed the office space to be its own cubicle. To her right, against the west wall was a piano that had cleaner keys than she had ever seen. A bookcase filled in the corner space just on the other side of the piano. The south wall had an entertainment center with a forty-inch screen TV flaunting itself on top and a VCR player in a cubby just underneath. A case overflowing with DVDs lay just in between the edge of the entertainment center and a French sliding glass door. Blue faded carpet that matched the carpet in the dining room served as a rug.

"So, this is our family room! Lots of cuddling and movies in here." Kate squeezed Anja's right arm. "Not as much work." She laughed as she pointed toward the office.

She then led Anja in a 180-degree rotation, and Anja noticed that the walls were varying shades of blue from sky to navy and even a mix. After they stepped over the threshold, they looked into the kitchen with light wooden cabinets and an island with manufactured granite on top that matched the other counters. And Kyle, of course. He stood in the left corner where the stove was. With an oven mitt on each hand, he turned around and winked at Kate.

Both women saw it. But only one truly appreciated it.

They proceeded to walk past the library that adjoined the kitchen and dining room with open archways. The front door stood erect to their right as they headed toward the hall.

"Sunshine!" It was Kyle calling them for dinner.

"Coming, Ray!" Anja embraced the close proximity to her new friend as she placed her hand over Kate's. The hand that had remained there since they considered going on a tour.

She felt comfortable enough asking, "Ray? You told me his name is Kyle!" Both of them laughed out loud before Kate explained.

"He started calling me his sunshine because he says I am always happy and full of life. But I wanted him to be a part of that, so I started calling him Ray because I am the sunshine and he is my sunray." Kate's face scrunched up as she realized how cheesy it sounded. But Anja didn't mind.

They backtracked five feet until they found the open kitchen and dining room. Kyle had set the table with Dixie paper plates and paper bowls, plastic red Solo cups, and plasticware. A big porcelain bowl was in the center of the table on a hot pad next to a bouquet of an assortment of red and white roses. She saw the steam coming from the top of what Kyle said was a shepherd's pie. Apparently, it was a layered pie from green beans to mashed potatoes to ground beef to cream of chicken soup.

They all sat down in the ladder chairs that held blue and white floral cushions. Kate sat next to Anja and across from Kyle.

After a blessing on the food, Kyle offered his hand and dished up pie to Anja, then Kate, and then himself.

"So, how long have you been living in Lemon Grove, Anja?" She extended her index finger as if to silently ask for a moment while she also tried to not choke on her food. Kyle chose the perfect time to ask her a question.

After hurriedly chewing and swallowing, she replied, "I have been in this area most of my life. When I was eighteen," which she spoke in quieter and rushed tones, "I moved down here into my parents' vacation home after they passed. I just had to get away."

"I'm sorry, Anja. I didn't mean to bring up painful memories." Anja appreciated Kyle's gesture, but she needed to face it.

"Don't worry, Kyle. It is good for me to talk about it. I'm still not ready to talk about the details, but one day we will get to that point. I think that SJ would really enjoy your company." She looked down at her food as if she would see him there before looking into Kate's crystal-blue eyes. "And I know he would appreciate all that you have done for me."

"Oh, Anja. It is our pleasure. We just moved here a few weeks ago, and I have been wanting to make new friends. I think that the Lord put you in our path, and I am so grateful that He did!" Anja couldn't help but smile. After all, Kate was right about all of it, especially about God's hand in it. He had been there every step of the way, even when she was talking to SJ about him leaving to serve, even when she felt utterly alone. But she wasn't. Not really. Jesus Christ had paid the price so she would never have to be alone. Never. And He was there through friends, such as Kate and Kyle.

Father, I am so sorry that I forgot. I am so sorry that I got so caught up in my world, in my life, that I forgot that You are there, that You always have been, that You always will be. Please help my heart truly change so that I can see You, so that I will trust You no matter what. Thank You so much for reaching out to me through Kate and Kyle. Thank You for reminding me of Your hand in my life, even if I cannot see it all the time. I love You, Father. In the name of Jesus Christ, amen.

Kate waited while Anja finished her prayer. She knew what it was like to want to talk to Him right then and there. She did the same thing, something that Kyle finally got used to and came to admire about her. She never put her relationship with God on hold.

Once Anja opened her eyes and looked up once again, Kate smiled. "What were you thinking about?"

"God is oh *so* good." Anja returned the smile, and Kate could see it. The Holy Spirit walked in. She felt Him enter, knew that He had needed a moment with Anja and was grateful she and Kyle could witness it.

"Yes, He is." There was a moment of silence as the three of them soaked in the Spirit's presence, peace, and love that filled their souls. It was like all of the holes inside of her were being healed, mended, and filled with a love that only came from Him.

"So, how did you two meet?" Anja always loved those stories. They reminded her of God's hand in others' lives, in the possibility of a happily ever after despite the war, the news, and the darkness that seemed to be suffocating the world.

Kyle gestured to Kate to share the story; there was no mistaking who loved to tell it more.

"Well, I actually met Kyle"—she reached across the table and grabbed his hand—"when I was a student at Utah State. His brother was in my class, and we became good friends," seeing the confused and worried look on Anja's face, Kate quickly continued, "but it was nothing more than that. He was more like the younger brother that I never had. One night, he invited me over to game night with his family. I didn't have any plans—"

"Which was surprising because my brother always said that she was busy, that she had other plans, so it was a shock to see her walk in the door that night." His teasing smile only made the moment even better.

"Anyway, I went over and had a lot of fun! It was the best game night I had ever been to. The last game we played was spoons, and it came down to Kyle and I." She raised her hand as if to reassure her audience that everything would work out. "And I *won!*"

"Yes, after you shoved me to the side so that my shoulder rammed into the couch." Kyle laughed at the memory as he rubbed the part of his shoulder that hugged the couch a bit too hard.

"It's not my fault you got in the way." She showed all of her teeth and then teased, "And you have been ever since."

"Oh, that is it!" He let go of her hand, and in two swift steps, he was behind Kate tickling her sides.

After she found herself on the floor and out of breath, Kyle took a step back to gloat in his accomplishments. Anja was right there with him laughing at Kate's expense.

Kyle's face slowly turned into a tomato when he finally noticed that Anja had seen that. "Sorry."

"No worries!" Anja was still laughing.

"So, Anja, tell us more about yourself. How did you meet SJ?"

A smile spread across her face that she couldn't control. "We met at Little Caesars. He held the door open for me, and I just knew." She looked out the window that was at the end of the table as if replaying the scene outside in the rain that had just started to spring to life. "I knew that he was special." Moments went by as Kate and Kyle let her reminisce.

"Where is he now?" It didn't bother her that Kate hadn't told Kyle everything about their conversation earlier. Actually, it was nice that she was able to share it. Even if it hurt.

"He is overseas fighting in the marine corps." A look passed between Kyle and Kate that didn't go unnoticed by Anja. It was familiar, but she couldn't quite pin it down. Not wanting to push boundaries, she explained, "He left soon after we got married, actually."

"Ooh!" Kate clapped her hands together repeatedly. "Tell us the story, please?" Kate looked like a little girl whose dad just told her they were going to read her favorite bedtime story. Again.

"Maybe it is a good thing he isn't here right now. He gets embarrassed when I tell it, but he doesn't have a say this time." She wanted to dance, to go back in time, to replay that scene with him, but telling it would suffice. She scooted to the front of her seat, ready. "It started when he said 'Marry me!'" Her theatrics had helped, since Kyle and Kate were leaning forward, waiting for more.

She couldn't help but build up the suspense, so she let the silence linger a little longer.

"Then...?" It was Kyle.

"Then I said yes!"

Kate chimed in, "That can't be it!" She shook her head, not accepting it.

"Okay! So, he did say that. It was just after he told me he was going to join the marines. It was actually really hard, and I didn't want to let him go, but I trusted him with the Lord. After I did that, I felt better. I was at peace. I got so excited I wanted to fly up through the clouds with him, and yell *yes* for all the world to hear, not to show off or to rub it in others' faces, but to share my happiness with everyone. I wanted to show everyone that needed some light in their eyes that God is real, that He has a plan, even if we don't quite expect it.

"So, I was going to say yes, of course, but not until he asked me properly." She laughed as she remembered the terrified look that had initially crossed his face when she corrected him. "I made him get on one knee and ask me the way I deserved." She shook her hands back and forth as if to keep their attention, which wasn't needed since she had all of it. "Not that I deserve more or better, but I was selfish and wanted it done that way." She grew quieter as a sliver of sadness seeped in. "And he did. He treated me like a princess and got on one knee."

She gestured toward the ground as if he was right there on one knee in front of her. "He kept the prelude simple, which was fine with me since I had been dying to say yes from the moment I first laid eyes on him." She twisted the ring that had a single diamond in the center of the band that displayed roses. "'Anja Rose Whittle, my love, will you marry me?' I said yes and jumped into his arms. I was so happy that I forgot about the ring!" All of them joined in a chorus of laughter as the memory and image brought a lightheartedness to the room. The sadness was still there, in her heart; it always would be, but with Kyle and Kate, she saw God working in her life.

She saved her wedding story for another time to give herself room to clean up dinner. Her parents were gone, but they did teach her the value of cleaning up after herself, especially when at others' houses. Afterward, Kyle and Anja moved back to the dining room table while Kate went into the family room to grab a game.

I know you know that I'm not telling the truth! The Psych theme song was playing, which meant one thing: her phone was ringing. "I am so sorry. I thought I put this on silent." Kyle waved it away, not worried that she needed to take the call. She walked toward the hall as she put the phone up to her ear. That's where she saw Kyle, in a picture on the wall, in a marine uniform.

A cry from her phone brought her back. "Oh, hi, Mama!" She hadn't always been good at answering the phone, but she was trying to get better so she could be there for her in-laws, in case they needed her.

All she got in return were muffled sobs, the kind when someone is trying to hide that they are crying, but there was no mistaking it this time. She had heard it within herself too many times.

"Mama?" She didn't see Kate walk into the living room holding Farkle. She didn't see her sit on Kyle's lap. She didn't see them kiss. "Mama!" She didn't mean to yell; it just came out.

And all she heard Rebecca choke out was, "He's gone."

12

The Void

Thump-thump. All she could see was SJ lying on the table. *Thump.*

She knew it wasn't him, but he definitely got his looks from his dad. It was too real. Too much. Twelve seconds too many.

She looked away as she wrapped her arms around Rebecca. She had nothing to say to take away the pain, to ease the heartache, to heal the scars. And yet, she knew what it was like to lose the person she loved the most on Earth. She knew what it was like to pray and to hope and to dream for more, for better. And she knew what it was like to understand that things would never be the same again. But she wasn't the only one.

Father in heaven, Why? I know I said I wouldn't ask You that. I know. But I don't exactly feel guilty. I'm sorry. Should I? I just... I can't, Father. I can't understand it. I don't understand. Why him? Why now? I have lost both of my fathers now. I can't lose any more. No more men in my life. That's it. You have two of them. I know. I know You have a plan. But I want to know. I need to know, Father. Why take Johnny? Father...

She couldn't finish.

I watched her holding her mom. Wearing the same black jeans and blue blouse she had worn to the Richardson's, she held on. She hoped Rebecca wouldn't mind having her snot on her new, soft, floral shirt.

She was taught that God had a plan, that He was in control, that He knew what He was doing. She wasn't so sure anymore, not as the image of her deceased father-in-law solidified itself in her brain.

She wasn't sure she wanted to see his body. Actually, she didn't want to see his body. But she couldn't let Rebecca do it on her own, and it would give her a chance to see him one more time. Looking back, she didn't need to see him one more time. Because it wasn't him.

True, his hair had gray specks now, but the chocolate was still there. It was the curly cocoa she saw in SJ's hair. True, his nose came to an abrupt point as it hovered over his mouth, but it was the nose she nudged as she and SJ shared kisses. True, his eyes looked gold when the sun hit them just right, but those were the eyes she gazed into as she fell into SJ's soul. True, his body was muscular, built, taken care of, despite the current ashy, sunken look, but it was SJ's frame with his toned muscles and healthy, youthful body. Yes, it was Johnny's body. But she still saw SJ.

She couldn't hold them back as the tears fell, further soaking Rebecca's shirt. She didn't even try to hold back her vocal outpouring of anguish.

But she was the only one making noise, the only one vocalizing her pain, the only one that appeared to be reacting. She took a deep breath and then stepped back while holding onto Rebecca's shoulders.

Rebecca not only looked pale, but she looked like her husband—lifeless, soulless. Even though blood was pumping in her veins, she was gone.

"Mama?" She leaned down a few inches so she could look directly into her eyes. "Mama!" Her heart started to beat faster as any glimpse of control she had continued to fade into nothing. She wrapped her arms around Rebecca and walked her through the mortician's office, where Dr. Hutch was sifting through papers as she tried to give the family space, to the nearest bench that was just outside the office. "Mama, let's sit down. Okay?" Still, Rebecca said nothing. So Anja held on tighter, rocking her from side to side. "I'm right here, Mama. Stay with me. It's okay. The Lord has a plan." She knew at least Rebecca would believe it. Moments passed in still more silence. "Mommy!"

And then she could see her, her birth mother—Reva Evangeline Whittle. But she didn't look like she usually did.

Every inch of her clothing latched onto her skin as the sweat and blood served as glue. Her abdomen continued to retract and expand in huffs of strained air. Daddy was there too sitting behind Mommy. But he was already gone. The blood running from a gash in his head confirmed her fear.

All she could think of was that it was her fault.

"Anja?" It wasn't until then that she realized she had been crying again.

"Mama!" She squeezed her mother-in-law, not wanting to let go. If she did, she might be gone for good, like Mommy and Daddy and now Johnny.

"Honey, what's wrong?" She couldn't help but laugh. No matter what, her mother-in-law always seemed to remember there were more people than just her.

"Besides you-know-what?" She saw the sadness surface again, but just as quickly, Mama stored it long enough to listen to Anja.

"I just don't understand, Mama. He has taken almost everyone from me. And I can't take it anymore. I really don't think I will make it if I lose even one more person."

With understanding in her eyes, she responded, "You mean SJ." There was no question.

"Yes!" New tears surfaced as the fear crept in. "Don't get me wrong, Mama. I can't lose you either." She gazed into Rebecca's eyes. "But he looks just like him." Now it was Rebecca's turn to shed tears. She understood that it seemed as if they were losing both of them at the same time. True, it was Johnny's body that rested on the table, but SJ's body wasn't any closer to them.

"I know, baby. I know." Rebecca untangled from underneath Anja's embrace and proceeded to wrap herself around Anja. No, she couldn't save her heart. No, she couldn't control where her son went or where he was. However, she could control what she did right then, so she wrapped her arms around her baby and held on.

After several moments, Anja spoke up. "Mama, what happened?" Since leaving the Richardson's in a hurry on her way to the hospital, she hadn't had time to get any updates.

Rebecca sucked in a deep breath, keeping her chin on top of Anja's head as she ran her fingers through her hair. "He got an infection in his foot, which was treated two days ago." She could feel Anja look up at her, realization dawning.

"That's why you were out of town this weekend." All Rebecca could do was nod.

"He was transferred here yesterday, but something happened in between, and his lungs filled with blood. They tried to stop it and did…" Sobs kept her from continuing. Anja just waited with a clamped lip, part of her not wanting to know what finally took him away from them. "But he had a heart attack earlier this evening…" She couldn't finish. And it didn't matter. Anja knew the end.

This wasn't supposed to happen. It wasn't fair. None of it was. SJ being away. Johnny being gone. Just Anja and Rebecca left to fend for themselves. So, it was as good a time as ever.

Father in heaven… She took a deep breath. *I know that I asked why earlier. And I still want to know. I do. Tonight wasn't supposed to end this way. This isn't when Johnny was supposed to return to You. Mama says You have a plan, and I think I believe it. Maybe. I just don't see it. I can't see what good this will bring, especially with SJ gone. He isn't even here. And what if he…* God knew what she couldn't say.

Anja, I am here with you.

So, Lord, please, please give Mama and me peace. Please let us see what You have planned, what we are supposed to do next. Because I don't know where to go from here. Father, I need You. She tried to hide herself even more in the protection of Rebecca. *And, Father, please, please keep SJ safe. Please help him come home to us. Please, Father. I know You have faith in me, that You aren't supposed to give us more than we can take, but I cannot live through losing SJ too. Lord, I can't take anymore. Please strengthen us and help us to grow closer to You, to better understand and appreciate Your Beloved Son's Atonement. In the name of Your Son, Jesus Christ, amen.*

She determined that all she could do was lean on Him, the One who knew her more than anyone else, the One who loved more deeply and passionately than anyone else, the One who somehow knew what was best for her, for Mama, for SJ, even for Johnny.

The peace started to fall. Slowly. With each deep breath she took while in her mama's arms, it came. Until it occurred to her that she had no idea how she was going to tell SJ.

13

The Black

He could touch her. He could just reach out and feel her smooth skin underneath his rough fingertips. He could run his fingers along the white tulle that gracefully covered the white silk as it perfectly draped her body. He could twist her dirty-blonde, short, glimmering hair in his fingers and laugh as it just slipped right out of his grasp. He could follow the bone structure of her face with his fingers. He could hold her face, teasingly pinch that button nose of hers, kiss those plush lips of hers, get lost in those ocean eyes of hers. And it was all thanks to Him.

They knelt together before God and their friends and family just that afternoon. Words were exchanged. Covenants were sealed. The reception was unforgettable too. But his favorite part was when he woke up thirteen hours later to a beautiful morning—beautiful solely because she was there, where he could hold her. So he did as he remembered.

The salty water teased the cream sand that stretched out in front of them as the sun hid behind a few thin clouds. The view seemed to go on for miles. He reached out and grabbed his wife's hand as they walked barefoot down the sandy runway.

It was definitely a God-thing that no one else was there. He could feel her next to him as he ran his thumb along her thumb, letting her know he was there, that he would never leave her.

He couldn't stop staring at her. He had been doing it all day, and he never wanted to stop. It was truly the best day of his life. It was what he had only dreamed about since he realized she was what he wanted, what he needed: someone to love more than anyone on earth, someone to care about more than himself, someone to cherish. Anja was that someone. Anja would be that someone for eternity.

He looked over as they walked in silence, soaking in the moment. Her hair was in what she called a waterfall braid with an occasional baby's breath strand in it. Not a single speck of makeup dotted her face. She had told him earlier that she wanted to love herself just the way she was, the way she would look after she died. She wanted to be herself at all times. It was just one more thing that captured his heart and made him hold on as tight as he could.

Dear Heavenly Father, thank You for Your love. Thank You for helping Anja and me find each other. Thank You for trusting us with each other. And thank You so much for her, for all of her. In the name of Jesus Christ, amen.

"SJ?" He noticed that her eyes looked at him with more love than he had ever seen.

"Yes?" He knew he was busted, so there was no reason to act innocent.

"Where were you?" One side of her mouth lifted as her eyes sparkled.

"Lost in you." Yes, he was flirting. Yes, he was teasing. But no, he wasn't joking.

Her lips curled up as she tried not to show how much in love she was with him, not that it helped because both of them knew. "Funny that!" Her eyebrows bounced up as they invited a challenge.

"Funny how?" He cocked his head, bracing himself for what was to come.

"Funny because I was lost in myself too." She lost it as she leaned over and slapped her knee, proud of herself, and to be honest, he was proud of her too. I mean, he had been waiting to hear that she was lost in herself, that she loved herself almost as much as he did, if not even more so. He pulled her to his body as both of them continued to laugh.

"SJ!" He wasn't ready for that, not to hear Phillipe. Phillipe wasn't even there when they got married.

His eyes opened to gaze into the faces of his team. Even Sergeant Declan Brooklyn, the redheaded new guy, was there. They hadn't had much time to get to know each other, not after being sent out again with orders to serve a mission dependent, so he wouldn't be going anywhere until the mission was accomplished.

It all came back. Well, some of it. The last thing he remembers was the loudest noise he had ever heard. He and his team were driving to the next city on their outlined route in order to clear the area of all enemies, but they never reached the city—not the one they were expecting.

Fragments of the vehicle with a sprinkling of dust, sweat, and blood caked all of them, some from their heads to their toes.

"Hey, man!" As his focus shifted, it dawned on him that each of them had chains attached to their right ankles.

"What happened?"

"There was an IED." Phillipe used a very low volume. "We dragged you out of the Motor T just before it exploded." Phillipe shook his head. SJ wanted to scream. He wanted to punch the wall. He wanted to do something, anything, but he couldn't.

"They were ready, man." Phillipe brought him back. Again. SJ furrowed his eyebrows, trying to read Phillipe's mind, knowing it hurt him to go back. "They came out of nowhere, and the next thing we know, we are here in this bunker, and no one on our side knows where we are." Phillipe shook his head.

"God does." Some believed; most didn't. But that didn't matter to SJ right then. All that mattered was that he believed that God knew, that God was the only One who could get them out.

Dear heavenly Father, this was certainly not what I had planned for today or for this mission. Ever, really, so could you please, please help us find our way home? Please help us make it back. All of us, Father, please. I'm counting on You. I love You. In the name of Jesus Christ, amen.

It came with more force and volume than anything he had heard from Him before. *I am here, son. And I love you more.*

Despite the circumstances, he laughed. He actually laughed. Only God could make him laugh at a time like this, playing a God-card SJ knew he could never beat. But all teasing aside, he knew it to the depths of his soul. No matter the cinder blocks that surrounded them at every turn. No matter the wet air that threatened to suck the oxygen right out of their lungs. No matter the gunk that clung to their bare feet, skin, and the scraps of their clothing. No matter their next second could be one or all of their finales. Because He was there. And He loved SJ and every single other man in that room. No matter what.

14

The Release

Today would be the day to let go, to take a step forward. She couldn't do anything about SJ's absence, about his unknown whereabouts but pray. And pray harder. But she could also control this.

She leaned down and unlaced her tennis shoes. No more waiting. She saw them every day. But today, in the dirt of the dairy, she would unveil them in a place where she was comfortable, a place that brought her peace every time she stepped onto the property. Before she could, Jake shaded her feet as he leaned against her. It felt like a sign; she wasn't ready.

She couldn't help but laugh as she clenched her teeth. She just wanted to pick him up, squeeze him, hold him, and give him kisses. But that wasn't his style. Besides, he was too big for that now. After fourteen pounds, she learned to adjust to not picking him up as often. But he was still good at knowing when she needed him even more than usual. She arched her back as she encompassed his tall, long body in her arms. She kissed the top of his head, right where the black becomes a tint of red. The dirt on his fur no longer bothered her taste buds.

"Thank you, handsome!" She patted his side as she rose again. "Good boy!" She was really impressed. There were cows, bulls, heifers, and calves spread out before them, but he was showing off that he could behave when it counted the most—not that biting at the vacuum as she tried to clean the carpets necessarily counted as misbehaving; it was just Jake being Jake. And she appreciated it, more than he would ever know.

After the two-mile run to the dairy, she didn't want to do much more running until she was headed back home. Johnny used to come to this dairy, usually on Thursdays. He wasn't there this time, nor would he be in person ever again, but she knew he was there in spirit. He loved the cows too much. So, there she was with Jake. Both of them needed a break. The wedding she had been planning was coming up really soon, and she was really excited. It was for one of Kate's friends. They were getting married on May 19, 2019. Only seven days away.

Which was even more reason to take a break. Jake needed a break from taking breaks. He may have Shepherd in his blood, but he loved sleeping an awful lot. She couldn't blame him. It was a dream life, and if she couldn't have it, she loved that he could.

But she couldn't take a step forward. Not even one.

Anja... She knew exactly what He wanted her to do.

Father, You know I can't. I'm not ready. She shook her head, almost laughing at His timing.

Oh, Anja, you know you can. Through My Beloved. With Him. Please, stop running. She knew He didn't mean to physically stop running. He was pleading with her to stop running away from Him, from His protection, from His forgiveness. She didn't usually. She wanted Him more than anything. But not here, not when she didn't deserve it. He may know everything. But He had one thing wrong.

Daddy. She was hoping using that term would help Him to better understand. *You know I don't deserve it. I can't be forgiven. Even You can't let this go.* She plopped on the ground as she crossed her legs in front of her. Jake made a 360-degree turn before sitting right next to her, nudging her elbow with his long black nose. She wrapped her right arm around his body as she leaned on him. *They are gone because of me.*

Who am I? She sat up straight. That wasn't Him. That couldn't be Him. He knew exactly who He was. Right?

I... I don't understand.

Anja, who am I? Each word held a pause. And then she heard it. The part of the question she didn't want to hear. *Who am I to you?*

Daddy... She couldn't continue. The tears took over. It was better that way. At least for now. Manure remnants and hay dust collected in her nose as she tried to inhale more oxygen. Poor Jake. He was used as her tissue yet again, but he didn't mind. At least not that he showed.

I love you, Anja. I always have. I always will. No matter what. She cupped her face with the palms of her hand as she tried to hide her face from everyone and everything. He was right. He was always right.

But I left You. You let me rip their lives apart. You let me take my shoes off. You let me drive that day. You let me kill them. Silence. He didn't have anything to say. But she did.

I was so happy. Life was perfect. It couldn't have been a better day. We were headed to celebrate that I was going to college. I had made it through high school, on to bigger and better things. And I was on board with You. We were unstoppable: You and I. She had to take a deep breath. *But then, You left me when I needed You the most. Why didn't You warn me?* She shook her head. *I know. You don't have an answer for that still, but that is why I left You.*

Words came as she had enough air to fuel them. *And You stayed away. For way too long. Why?* She picked up a gray stone near her and threw it toward the cornfield that bordered the dairy.

No longer could she hear the teeth against metal as the cows chewed on the fence. No longer could she feel the sweat drip down her back. No longer could she smell the fresh, concentrated manure. *Daddy, You took everything from me! I just wanted to enjoy a dinner with my parents to celebrate my future. But instead, I lost everyone I loved in one single evening.*

It took me a year to find You again. But it wasn't until I was ready to forgive You, to let You take control. But I can't let it go. I can't even look at my feet, Father. The feet that ruined my life. She took a deep breath and leaned back, burying her hair in the dust on the cement sidewalk that cradled the cow pens. No more tears came.

Lean not on your own understanding...

In all my ways acknowledge You, and You will direct my paths. She knew that by heart. Her parents taught it to her when she was young.

But they were gone.

She slowly sat up, noting that Jake had never left her side. As she did, it played like a movie in her head—her driving, the dinner, the car accident, the loss of her parents, her year off school, the move to southern California, UCSD being lenient and letting her start a year later than planned, her living in her parents' empty house, her anguish, prayers, pain in that house, her waiting for that something, that someone that would make her feel better, her finding Him again, realizing she was missing Him. And of course, then she found SJ.

It all added up. One followed the other, perfectly planned by Him. He had been there the whole time. Even when she couldn't see Him. And it wasn't Him who took her parents from her. It wasn't even her. That was beyond her control. No matter what she thought of her involvement, of her place in the blame.

Daddy... This time, it was her that understood, truly understood, that He was her Daddy, even if she refused to read her scriptures, to pray, to go to church, to talk about God, to think about God, even if she spent a year wanting nothing to do with Him.

He was the One who helped her to find her mother's scriptures. He was the One who encouraged her to open up the book, to read its words, to read His words. It was the same book her parents had read to her every night when she was younger. It was the book she read on her own as she grew up to be prepared for anything that would come, for while it was accounts of those who had lived before her, those who had suffered before her, God continued to amaze her with how it applied to her even today. He was the One who fought for her when no one else would. He was the One who sought her when no one else would. He was the One who held her every single time she needed Him to. He was the One. Always had been.

And He was ready, waiting for her—a broken soul.

Daddy, I'm so sorry.

I forgive you, daughter. You are Mine. And I love you. That's right! She was His! She was His daughter! No matter what she had done, said, thought, she was His. And He wanted her. Still.

I am Yours, Father. Now and for eternity. I remember now. I remember all of it. Even the promises I made to You, to SJ. Thank You, Father. Thank You. I love You, Daddy. SJ knew she had left Him, but he didn't know how much she had been bottling it up inside of her.

For the first time in what seemed like a long time, she smiled. It was a smile that showed that she knew she was loved by Him, Who had never left her. She knew she was free. She jumped up onto her feet, ready for anything. Because right then, she really knew He was there. It was more real than the air she breathed. *Father, please, please help me give this peace and love to others. Please help me share You with others. Please lead me to do Your will, to help people who need You just the way I need You. Please. I love You and I always will. In the name of Jesus Christ, amen.*

Jake slowly stood up and wagged his tail, also ready for anything.

I know that you know that I'm not telling the truth! She pulled her phone out of her side pocket.

"Hey, Kate! How are you?" There was no response on Kate's end. "Kate, are you there?"

"Anja, can you come over please?" Then the line went dead. She couldn't even tell her that she couldn't be there for another hour. She would skip the shower, but she had to run back.

An hour later, she pulled into Kate's driveway. Jake jumped off the passenger seat and out the driver's door the second she was out of the truck.

She led him up to the front door after a few stern vocal redirections. The door flew open before she had a chance to knock. She caught Kate as she fell into her arms, taking both of them down to their knees.

After moments of holding her, she pulled back just enough to brush the damp hair out of Kate's face. Kate looked up with red-stained eyes.

"They took him, Anja. They took Kyle."

15

The Soul

His face, along with the faces of all of his team, no longer looked familiar. They all held a darkness, a black that couldn't be wiped off, no matter how hard they tried. It was permanent after just three weeks. A mix of sweat, what smelled like tar, blood, and burnt skin layered their faces, hiding everything, including the person underneath. Cheekbones, knees, and elbows were starting to poke out a little more. Even their ribs were making an announcement. But they couldn't do anything about it. They had tried.

He busted through the door in the middle of the wall wearing a black mask, a black sweater, black pants, black boots, and holding an M16 A4 rifle. SJ's M16 A4 rifle. He aimed the weapon at SJ and his team.

"Stand up!" His accent was thick and foreign, but there was no mistaking what he said. Not that there was any room for mistakes. Private Damian Munoz grabbed onto Private Day's shoulders, or what was left of them, as Day reached out and grabbed Munoz's arms, steadying themselves as they willed themselves to rise. Lance Corporal Wheeler, Private First Class Deeks, and Sergeant Bates gripped the grimy concrete walls, hoping they would be able to stand, but most importantly, hoping they would stay standing. Lance Corporal Alexander looked at Lance Corporal Gensicki, who also used the wall, and smiled as he crawled over to Sergeant Brooklyn, grabbed underneath his arms, and helped him up.

Brooklyn learned the hard way to stay standing in their presence. He was harshly dragged out of the room to receive multiple jolts to the chest in the bunker next door and then was pushed, or kicked, whichever way got him back faster. He was still trying to recover.

After all of them were standing, he smiled, the kind of smile that indicated he knew his next target.

"You!" He pointed at Phillipe. SJ knew what that meant. And he didn't want it to happen again. None of his brothers would give answers, no matter how hard they tried to get answers.

"No!" Before thinking about it, SJ launched himself forward, interrupting Phillipe's path. He stumbled for a few steps, but just as quickly, he shakily stood as tall as he could, serving as a physical barrier between him and Phillipe.

His laugh was like none he heard before, like this was a treat.

Without any warning, not even from God, his right shin started to burn.

He didn't notice that Phillipe was flung out of their prison, landing harshly against the wall they hadn't seen in weeks. Nor did he notice four days later when Phillipe didn't come back. Because all he could think about was her, what she had said.

After a prayer together, she admitted, "SJ, I can't." She buried her face in her knees as she wrapped her arms around her legs and pulled them closer to her body. The breeze brushed her hair to the side, exposing the right side of her face. SJ could see the tears falling as they grazed her cheeks and lightly spotted her jeans. He loved her in those jeans; they extenuated her curves perfectly. It was just a reminder of how much he loved her, not just her heart, her humor, her personality, but also her body—all of her.

Using his hands, he inched closer to her so he could wrap his left arm around her. He ran his hand up and down her arm as he started to softly hum "You are my sunshine." After a few seconds of listening to him, she lifted her head. The slightest smile lit up her face. "You know me too well."

He shrugged and responded, "Or not enough." That is what he used to say. It was his way of saying that he knew there was more for him to learn about her, that she was a mystery he would spend eternity uncovering. "It's okay, love. Just talk about it when you are ready."

She shook her head. "What if I am never ready?"

"I will still be by your side." She found her gaze locked onto his. "Always." She started to cry again.

"It was right after my parents died." She told him about her parents' death while they were dating, but they hadn't touched that subject often since then. She knew she should have told him this part before they got married, but He reminded her that it couldn't wait any longer, so they walked in the dark to the lake, following the path illuminated by the moon. "I let God go. I walked away, expecting never to see, talk to, or hear from Him again." She took a deep breath but shook as she exhaled. "I hated Him." She didn't yell it, but the force behind her voice told him that it still rocked her. Even then.

"I just wanted to drive my parents to a nice dinner. It was my treat to them—the dinner, the chauffer, the whole evening. I wouldn't have been able to get through thirteen years of school without them." A tear fell down her cheek as she hid her mouth behind her shoulder. "They deserved that and so much more. I was ready to give them everything I couldn't before. Everything I didn't understand before. The Lord had blessed me more than I deserved." She closed her eyes but remained facing SJ. "But then He took everything from me." The anger from before was no longer in her eyes. A sorrow, a longing remained for her parents. But more that she had done things differently. And he had only seen that once since the day he met her.

He knew there was more, so he waited. "I always drove with my shoes off." His raised eyebrow caught her attention. "I know! I know! That isn't the safest way to drive, but it was the most comfortable. It was when I felt most in control." She paused, not for dramatics, but to gain her composure. "Until that night. I had driven my car so many times before. We had such a groove, but that night, those feet betrayed me. I had an itch on my foot." She shook her head, willing the memory to pass. "It wouldn't go away. I kept my eyes on the road and leaned down to take care of it. But my foot couldn't touch the pedals. Neither of them could." Her back arched as she tried to hold back sobs. "Probably because I saw the tree. And I swerved the wrong direction."

He wrapped both arms around her and pulled her to him. Her head fell perfectly onto his shoulder as she released tears that had been held for years. She curled her arms in front of her and clung to his shirt. Moments passed before she said anything more.

"I saw it all again tonight. In perfect clarity. It was too real, SJ." She sat up and looked up at him. Holding back more tears, she choked out, "I'm sorry."

"Oh, princess." He opened his heart, and she fell against him again. "I knew you would tell me when you were ready." She shook her head and sat up again. Reaching for his hands, she squeezed.

"I'm sorry for that. And for what happened next." She didn't look away. "I was so mad at God. I was so convinced that He left me, that maybe He wasn't there ever." She leaned closer. "I knew He was, but it didn't feel like it. Not then. So I walked away. I left Him because He left me first. Or I thought He did. No one could change my mind. I was so set on that choice.

"I threw out any religious documents or books I had ever owned. I sold my parents' house and moved into this vacation home, their vacation home. Within seconds, I promised myself to never pray again, to never read His words again. I ignored e-mails and phone calls from UCSD. I didn't care about anything and definitely not about anyone. Not even me.

"I even—" she stopped, not ready to continue. "I got so far away from Him, from life, that I grabbed the knife. I knew I wasn't going to use it to cut anything or to open anything. It was aimed for my heart. The heart that was so cold, so distant, so dead that I had no problem puncturing it. No problem putting an end to anything that was left inside. That is…"

"The scar you briefly told me about. The one that held a story you had never told anyone." His voice was soft, but she heard the fear. She tenderly placed her hand on top of his as he continued to soak in what she had just said. They didn't speak for several moments. She had come clean when she was ready. He honestly hoped it would have been addressed before they made promises, but he knew she didn't wait in an effort to abuse their trust. Still, he wasn't ready to hear that. He didn't mind as much that she had done it, for he knew she never would again, but the thought of losing her was too much.

She leaned forward and kissed his forehead, lingering there for a few extra moments. He breathed in deeply, praying the moment would last forever, just the two of them on the lake shore.

"It is my one regret in life, SJ. There is no going around that. I shouldn't have let myself go that far. I shouldn't have let Him go. I mean, He never let me go. But I was too ready to just leave Him in my dust." She grabbed both of his hands and looked into his soul. "Please, please, SJ, never let Him go. Never walk away from Him. Never forget that He is there for you every step of the way, that He loves you more than anyone ever will." A smile grew on her face. "Even more than me."

He knew it was true. After he and his parents found God, they made a pact to never leave Him, to always trust Him. It was even truer and more powerful as he looked into her eyes. All doubt and pain were gone. All he saw was her soul, one so rooted in God there truly was no going back. Only forward, closer to God. He could see her running to Him for the rest of eternity. And he wanted to be there, right next to her, holding her hand the whole way.

Until now. He didn't know if he could run to someone Who wasn't there, someone Who hadn't been there in weeks, someone Who may not have ever been there. But she didn't have to know. Besides, what did it matter?

16

The Light

She didn't say anything. Neither did Kate. How do you say you are sorry? How do you say you wish that Kyle wasn't redeployed, that he wasn't taken from his wife, that he wasn't where he was? Wherever that was! How do you say that you know what it feels like? But you also know that won't help. Nothing will until he comes home. If he comes home.

She sat there as she held Kate in her arms. She didn't care as her tears started to mingle with Kate's. It had been sixteen seconds since she last thought about it, but she still thought about it every day. He was still gone. After three years and seven months, she didn't know if he was coming back. Of course, she still hoped he would, but she wouldn't expect anything. She couldn't.

Father, I know You have a plan for me, for Kate, for Kyle, for SJ. I know that, but honestly, it is hard to see. I don't see Your plan. And I certainly don't feel it. Nothing feels right. Nothing feels safe. I mean, even after being home for years, Kyle was taken away from Kate. Yes, he is in the reserves, but that doesn't mean he was supposed to be deployed. Not after all this time. And not now, Father.

I need Him, Anja. She straightened her back immediately.
Father, I didn't mean that...

I need you to trust Me. Please. She was growing familiar with Him asking that of her, so why did she still struggle with it?

Okay, Father. I will. Always. And please help me do better at it.

I am here. Always. I love you, Anja. More tears found their escape as the words hit her harder than they had before. She knew that He loved her, and He meant it. He loved everyone else just as much. It was more love that she could comprehend, more than she could see. But she knew without a doubt that it was real.

Not my will, Father, but Your will be done. She smiled as her heart pumped just slightly slower, as the sunshine shone slightly brighter, as she squeezed Kate, as He came to sit with them. *So, please keep SJ safe. Please keep Kyle safe. Wherever they are. Please help to heal Kate's heart. Please help her to recognize that You are still here, that You still love her, that Kyle is in Your hands, perfect hands.*

With the last two words, she coughed on her words as tears came stronger and faster. *Please continue to protect all of my loved ones, including Rebecca. Thank You that Johnny is with You. Please, please also heal Rebecca's heart. Please help me be Your light in the darkness that seems to be suffocating so many of us. We need You always, and now more than ever. Father, I love you. In the name of Jesus Christ, amen.*

He didn't respond. He didn't need to. He was there wrapping them up in His love in the way only He could.

Brushing her tear-soaked hair out of her face, Anja lifted Kate's head so she could see her crystal blue eyes. "Kate, stay with me. Keep breathing. One breath at a time." Understanding dawned in Anja's eyes as she continued. "Sometimes, that is all you can manage, and that is okay. Just don't stop." Pushing herself to a sitting position on the white tile floor in the hallway, Kate nodded. Without words, Anja linked her arms with Kate's and slowly stood. Jake followed her lead and stood with them after being curled up next to them.

"Do you mind if we pray together?" Kate just managed a nod of her head, so after Anja helped Kate get settled on their plush L-shaped blue couch and ensured Jake was behaving himself, Anja proceeded to offer her heart to God. After she concluded the prayer, she knew what she had to do.

A few hours later, she had dinner prepared. It was her grandma's chicken. Again. The oil at the bottom of the pan simmered as she pulled it out of the oven. The smell of parmesan and chicken filled her nose before she moved to stir the mashed potatoes. Mixed with butter, milk, cheese, and a hint of garlic, the potatoes looked like clouds. She wanted to jump up and down; it was the first time her potatoes had looked this good. Of course, it was when she didn't have SJ distracting her. After making sure the potatoes were still perfect, she turned the burner underneath the vegetables off. The chicken broth and salt had been absorbed, so she added butter for that element of creaminess. Seconds after she dropped the butter into the pot, there was a knock on the door.

Walking past the archway that led into the living room, where Kate sat watching videos of her and Kyle, she made her way to the front door. Opening it revealed Rebecca standing on the other side.

After introductions and filling their tall glasses and floral plates, the three women sat in the armchairs at the oval dining room table. There was no tablecloth. There had been, but that was before he was taken away; the tablecloth and the vase with red roses got the brunt of her frustration.

After a prayer on the food, Anja began, "So, I know it is hard, but we should get the rough stuff out of the way." She looked down at Jake, who was politely lying at her feet looking at her with big, brown, hopeful eyes, and smiled. "This is my favorite meal. I have made it several times. SJ always asked if I knew how to cook anything else. I would always promise that I could, but in many instances, there was no need: Grandma's parmesan chicken is just the perfect option. I made this for him on our third date. After the date, he said he was so impressed that he later confessed he almost proposed to me that night." She laughed at the memory, but it didn't last. "I miss him so much." The tears surfaced but didn't fall. "I haven't heard much from him over the course of three years, seven months, and thirteen days. Not that I am counting." That got all of them laughing, even if just a little. "It hurts, for sure. Every day." She nodded as she cut a piece of moist white chicken with the perfect crumble on top. "But I trust Him. Or at least, I am trying to. I am trying really hard to let go." She took a deep breath, avoiding eye contact because if she looked in their eyes, all she would see is a painful reflection.

Rebecca reached out to her left and enfolded Anja's hand in hers. Then she squeezed. "Well, it has been three months since

Johnny passed away, but I am doing better. There is no way to go back. There is no way to undo what has happened. All I can do is move forward with God leading the way. He has gotten me this far, and I know God will stay with me. No matter what." Her bottom lip quivered before she continued.

"And Johnny is there too. I can feel him with me, laughing at me when I forget to put the detergent in the washing machine, scaring me when he walks up behind me and kisses my cheek, holding me close while we waltz around the bedroom before we go to bed. All of it. Even our first disagreement rings in my head. I don't even remember what we talked about, but I do remember that it ended with us laughing so hard we cried. It wasn't like us to fight." A smile reached up to just below her eyes. "We never encountered another disagreement like that again." The smile finally touched her eyes.

"I wish I could have met him." It was Kate that spoke up.

"Me too." A chorus of laughter filled the room as Anja and Rebecca responded at the same time.

"Thank you for this." Kate gestured all around her. "For being here. For dinner." She picked up her plate and angled it as if advertising the chicken. But there was no chicken left, not even a crumb dotted the plate. She then put it down and took a deep breath. "For not leaving me alone. I have lived without him before. We did it for years when he was first deployed, but he assured me we wouldn't have to do that again after he came home. I know that isn't in his control, but it still hurts. A lot. I feel his absence more than I want to."

Anja laughed, but it was a laugh that breached as she recognized something. "I prayed. I prayed that I would know what to do to help those around me. I prayed for help to trust Him. I prayed for Him, every second." She let the tear fall. "And I want you both to know that He is there. And this is exactly where He wants us to be." She gently slapped the table. "So, I have an idea I want to run by both of you."

"Of course!" Kate's eyes lit up just for a moment.

"I want to start a support group. I want to reach out to other wives and mothers who need extra support, who need a reminder that God is there, that He is so good, that He is a God of so much love we can't even comprehend it!" With all of her, she knew that was what God wanted her to do next.

The room was quiet for a few moments.

"I'm in! We can read scriptures, pray together, and just talk. We don't make enough time to do that with all of the demands of life now, so I'm all in!" Anja knew Rebecca would have her back.

"Let's do it!" Kate's bright smile and firm nod confirmed her response. "We can hold it here if you want, or we can go to one of your houses, if you would rather." She shrugged.

"Here is perfect! Thank you." Anja leaned back in her chair and folded her arms, a glimmer in her eyes. "So, how did this all start?" She looked around her at Kate and Kyle's home.

Kate giggled that giggle when a girl is so in love there is no other way to describe it. "We met after I tripped him." The gasps encouraged her to speak a tad faster. "Don't worry! It was an accident. I dropped my phone on the floor while I was walking out of the gym, and he apparently wasn't paying attention because the next thing I knew, he was lying on his face on the cement. I had just graduated from college and moved back in with my parents while I tried to raise money to live, but I needed space. I need time to myself, so I decided to run it off at the gym." A deep, contemplative sigh escaped her lips. "And my life was forever changed." Cliché? Maybe little. But totally accurate.

The other women giggled at her comment, understanding the feeling. "We got engaged seven months later, on January 7, 2013. April 27, 2013, is the day we got sealed." Anja and Rebecca were quiet, letting Kate go back in time. "The proposal was amazing! He surprised me with a trip to the San Diego military hospital. After I found out he was a marine, I'll be honest, I was scared. Well, terrified. But I knew that God had called him to do that. I told him how I had always wanted to go to the hospital, to reach out. It was a longer drive, as we were both living in Arizona at that time, but it was worth it every time. We went a few times before, but he hadn't told me we were going that time. He apparently went earlier that week and planned the proposal with the staff. He even got my friends, Sergeant Gracie Risk and Private First Class Adella Maze to be in on it.

"They distracted me while he got others to hold up a sign that asked if I would marry him. Bud, another friend, was at one end holding the sign. That was the first time I saw Bud smile." Her gaze sunk a little. "After the explosion, he was paralyzed and didn't want to keep living, but he did because he hoped to find a purpose for his life. Anji was holding the other end of the sign. She was always smiling." Kate looked away for a split second. "Half of her face had been burned away in battle, and she was deaf in her left ear, but I loved to see her smile." Shaking her head, she continued, "Anyway, I said yes. But when I made promises to God and to Kyle four months later, I was happier than any other day of my life. A lot of brides say that, and so many mean it, including me. There really is nothing like loving someone so much you give him your eternity, your heart, your everything. We became one. I felt it. I wore my mother's dress and had a really inexpensive reception, but it was the most magical day of my life. I want to relive it every day." It was supposed to be a time of excitement, and it was. It always would be. But there was no way around the pain that day. "Especially now."

Anja reached out and held Kate's hand. Rebecca wrapped their hands in hers and squeezed.

I know you know that I'm not telling the truth! She excused herself and walked to the entry table next to the front door. It displayed a number from their area code, but it wasn't saved in her phone.

"Hello?"

"Mrs. Gensicki?"

"Yes?" She didn't like where this was going.

"Sorry to bother your evening. This is Master Sergeant Jay Beck from the United States Marine Corps. I have news regarding your husband."

"SJ? Is he okay? Where is he? Please tell me he is okay! Is he coming home?" She lifted onto her tippy toes, the excitement almost too much. She was louder than she expected; Rebecca and Kate were slowly walking toward her.

"Mrs. Gensicki, I'm afraid to inform you…"

17

---∘ ∘--

The Fight

"SJ, wake up! You can't go to sleep! Stay with me, soldier!" Private First Class Deeks lovingly slapped SJ's face, urging him to wake up. He had just gone to sleep, which wouldn't be bad if he hadn't taken a nap only minutes earlier. And if he wasn't bleeding internally. "Bates, we're losing him! Guys, I need you!" All five of them were already on their way.

The team, except for Phillipe, gathered around an unconscious SJ, waiting for further instructions.

"What do you need?" Bates got there first.

"I need him to wake up and to stay awake!" Munoz and Wheeler made it a point to take turns shaking him and slapping his face. "Bates, I need your knife." Bates didn't argue. He always had a spare knife that even they didn't catch. No one knew but his team. Handing it over despite the dents from the early failed attempts to escape, Deeks grasped it like his life depended on it. "Okay, I am going to make a seventeen-centimeter incision from north to south just below the bullet's entrance. And it is going to hurt. A lot."

Turning to Munoz and Wheeler, he said, "Keep trying! He has to be awake for this!"

"Why does his leg look black?" Day spoke up this time. "What exactly is wrong?"

Deeks turned to Day, who leaned over SJ. "It is called compartment syndrome. The bullet has moved and punctured the pretibial

85

artery, which causes a building of pressure. The blood is then compartmentalized and needs to be released. I wasn't worried about it, since the bullet seemed to be staying in place, but it moved. If we don't take care of this now and release the blood, he will die."

"Oh, is that it?"

"No! He will probably need to get it amputated when—"

"*Hey*, Munoz! Wheeler! What's up?" SJ was finally responsive. Well, kind of.

"SJ! Do you feel any pain?"

"Uh…not right now! What happened?" He closed his eyes tightly and then slowly opened them, trying to sit up.

"He is going numb to the pain. Hours in that condition can do that, but it isn't necessarily good. His nerves are shutting down, and soon he…"

"Will shut down." Bates didn't want to say it, but he had to make sure. Deeks's look confirmed it.

Turning to SJ, Deeks explained, "You were shot a few days ago. You were fine until the bullet moved. Long story short, I need to make an incision to save your life."

"Okay! I'm ready!" There he was. Ready for anything. He couldn't clearly see who was who, but he knew it was his team—the men he had stood by through pouring rain and scorching heat, the men who had defended him with all they had, the men he would live for as long as he had breath.

When he stood up for Phillipe, it was like a light bulb. He was there for them, for all the men in that room, and for all those back home: those he knew and those he would never meet. It was for them. So, he would do anything to bring his team home. No matter what.

"It is going to hurt, SJ. A lot." Deeks placed the knife against the risen black skin on SJ's right shin.

"Just do it!" He leaned his head back onto the ground. Munoz and Wheeler grabbed his hands. He didn't fight them but encompassed their hands in his. He needed them more than he wanted to admit, because he knew that if Deeks said it was going to hurt, it would hurt.

"Bates! Day! I need you to talk to SJ! Distract him!" He put little more pressure on the wound as Bates and Day asked SJ about his wife. They all knew about her. She was almost the only thing he talked about, besides God and his parents.

"You know, I—" Oh, he felt it! It was like carving into a lino-leum block. "You know? I feel it! I can definitely—" His chest rose as he started to limit the blood circulation of Munoz's right hand and Wheeler's left hand. It rose a few times as he gasped for air, and then he stopped moving.

"Welcome back, man! It's good to see you!" Deeks sighed and hung his head as he looked down at his lap. His arms were perched on his knees.

"Hey, man! Why does my leg hurt?" His voice was low, but not by choice.

"I had to cut it open to release the pressure buildup."

"Oh! Right!" SJ chuckled.

"Can you tell me where we are?" Deeks's tone was all-business. If he had a flashlight, he would check SJ's pupils, but that wasn't an option.

"When I find out where we are, you will be the first to know." Deeks nodded, acknowledging that SJ was conscious…and aware.

"Hey! Can you do me a favor?"

"Yeah, man! What do you need?" He sounded slightly drunk, but they all knew it wasn't from any kind of drink.

"I need you to tell me about this God person you believe in." No one else was awake.

"Uh…well, man. He… He, uh… He is…" SJ brought his hand to his forehead and rubbed it, wishing everything would go away. "He is God."

"That's all there is to it, folks! You got me! I want in!" SJ slowly tried to sit up, but Deeks pushed him back down onto the leg he extended so SJ could rest his head on it.

"Want in? To what?"

"Into your faith!"

SJ scrunched his eyebrows. "Really?"

u have given me nothing!" Both of them laughed,
, when SJ started to cough.

, just don't feel like I am in a position to talk about

, understanding, Deeks pushed, "Just tell me what you

"All right." He took a deep breath. "I know that I talked to Him
.nrough prayer. I would just open with His name, say what I wanted
to say, and then close in His Son's name. It was a way I coped with...
well, life. It was how I knew I would marry Anja one day. It was how
I knew to come here, to become a marine."

"Wow, man. Why did you listen?" SJ lifted his head. "Not to be
rude! I just can't imagine having someone tell me to risk my life and
leave my girl to end up here. Would God really ask you to do that?"

"I have been asking myself that same question, man." He let his
arm fall from his chest onto the wet floor.

"Are you allowed to do that? To question Him?" Deeks leaned
forward.

"I mean, yeah. We can do whatever we want. We call it agency:
the ability to choose. So I can do what I want, when I want, if I want.
But with agency comes accountability. So we are responsible for what
happens next, for our reaction." He paused halfway through stating
the last word. "And I reacted the way I said I never would. I pushed
Him away just when I needed Him the most. When He wanted
me to run to Him, I ran the opposite direction faster than I should
have." If he could have punched the air, he would have. "Oh, man!
I messed up!"

Deeks chuckled. "You lost me at 'reaction'!"

SJ shook his head. "I just lost sight of Him over these past few
weeks. I just couldn't understand that He would let me get this low,
that He would put us in this position. I mean, He asked me to come
here, but I didn't think 'here' would mean *here*." He briefly gestured
around, and Deeks more than understood.

"So, why are we here?"

"I don't know how to answer that. I don't even have the answer.
What I do know is that I trust Him. I forgot that until now, but I

do. He has gotten me this far. He brought me to Anja. He blessed me with the best parents. He blessed me with this team. I do know that He has a plan, and while I don't have all of the answers, He does. And that is okay with me. I don't"—he sucked in as much oxygen as he could, but it certainly didn't smell like oxygen—"need to know everything. I just need Him."

Deeks didn't know what to say. He hadn't heard anything like it. Nor had he met someone like SJ, someone who believed in a Being he couldn't see, in a Being he couldn't even just call on a phone, in a Being who would let them rot in an underground bunker. Alone. But then again, the idea couldn't hurt.

It was an idea that hinted at a light he hadn't seen in a while. There could be Someone who could hear them, Someone who knew where they were.

"SJ?" He nudged SJ with wide eyes. "SJ!" No response. Only shallow, infrequent breaths.

All Deeks could do next was pray. And hoped it worked.

18

The Doubt

"I need to talk to Master Sergeant Beck! Please! It is an emergency!" She was hanging out of her 1990 Chevrolet Blazer's driver window, waving at the marines standing guard of the east gate. One of them was in the booth just to her left. The other two were stationed in the middle of the gate—the gate that was still blocking her path.

She could see the helicopter garages about two miles ahead of her. She remembered looking at the eighteen helicopters, hearing words she would never think of again. But what was really engrained in her brain was that the helicopters were like her future. Big, full of possibilities, but looming and dark without him. They took him away. Maybe forever. And she never liked to think about it.

A marine wearing a beige and coffee uniform stepped out of the booth and approached her. "Ma'am, can you remind me of your name?" He leaned forward so his face was level with hers, but he maintained a professional distance.

"Anja Gensicki! I am SJ Gensicki's wife! He was sent away almost four years ago, and I don't know where he is! They said he is officially missing in action." She was talking so fast she forgot to breathe. She continued in haste, but she tried to find the peace that was deep inside her. "I just need to talk to Master Sergeant Beck!"

"You're SJ's wife? You are Anja!" The excitement in his tone soaked through his face.

"Yes! I am Anja!" There was an underlying question, but the marine quickly addressed it.

"He is my hero! He helped me adjust to life here. He took me in when I needed someone the most. And he introduced me to God." He shrugged with that last sentence, not wanting to make it a huge deal, but Anja knew what it felt like.

"That sounds like him!" Her smile dimmed just a little bit.

"I'm sorry, Anja." She gestured toward her. "May I call you Anja?"

"Oh, yes. Please do!" She flicked a tear away, hoping he wouldn't notice.

"They are going to do whatever it takes to find him, Anja. I promise. They even sent a team of reserves over to help with the search." She could only nod. He cleared his throat.

The radio crackled as he pushed the button and spoke into it.

"Yes, sir. Anja Gensicki. She needs to talk to you." He winced as he saw her listening intently. He politely smiled and turned to face away from her, but she could still hear him. "SJ Gensicki is her husband...okay, sir. I will."

Turning back around to face Anja, he reported, "He is waiting to see you." The gates started to open. "If you just drive straight through here, make the first left, then the first right, you will find a bunch of office buildings. His office building is the one in the middle. Go up to the second floor, turn left down the hall, and it will be the door right in front of you."

Following his directions, she stood in front of his door in less than ten minutes.

Father, please help me to hear You. Please help me be worthy of Your Spirit. Please help me show love. And please, please help us find SJ. In the name of Your Son, Jesus Christ, amen.

She knocked. "Come in!" His voice boomed through the door. It was a sound of control, authority. It didn't make the situation any better. Opening the door, she noticed his desk only a few paces in front of her. Made of cherry wood, his desk had a gloss finish. There were bookcases that bordered and accented the walls, but she only cared about the man sitting in the leather arm chair.

"Hello, sir!" He gestured for her to sit in the armchair that was opposite of his.

"Call me Jay, please."

"Sir, I need to know where SJ is. I need to know that he is okay. I need to know that my husband will come back to me." She couldn't hold back the tears, but she tried to control her shaky breathing.

He hung his head before he spoke. "Anja, we don't know where your husband is. We lost him and his team weeks ago and have not been able to pinpoint his location since. We have a team looking for him right now. When I know where he is, you will be the first to know." She shook her head, knowing that while this was how she pictured the conversation going, she didn't want it to actually go this way.

"Sir, with all due respect, please tell me what you know, what you actually know." He clasped his hands in front of him and rested them on the table.

"You are not authorized to know that information." She sat on the front edge of her seat and mimicked his hand position.

"Sir, I may not have the necessary clearance to know, but I think I am certainly more than authorized." She tried to smile at him. "My husband is missing. Only God knows where He is. And I have lived without him for almost four years now. I know that there is a chance that he is alive, but he has been dead to me for almost four years. Legally, I have a husband. But I don't know him anymore. I haven't talked to him in months. He no longer replies to my letters. And now I know why. All I ask, sir, is to know where he was last seen. It will be the first thing I know about my husband in months." There was only one word left to say. "Please."

He again politely and professionally refused, and she drove off the base feeling like she had just wasted time. After stopping by her house, she picked up Jake and headed to her third favorite place.

An hour later, she paid for parking, secured his leash, and rolled up her white capris. As she headed toward the beach, her pink blouse played with the wind and her dirty-blonde layered hair danced as she ran her fingers through it.

"Come on, handsome!" She didn't need to say it; he was already ahead of her. Sometimes she wished he could talk back. It would be better than his undecipherable barks. But he was there. She made a note to give him treats when they got back home. He had been really good with her coming and going a lot last week. She was with Rebecca and Kate scheduling times to meet, pondering people to invite, and discerning ways to advertise their support group.

Just before she allowed her sandals to collect sand, she slipped them off, securing them in the hand that wasn't holding the leash. She stopped and took a deep breath as the sand seeped through her toes and started to bury her feet in a natural massage. And she took a step. And another. The warmth radiated through her feet and up to her heart, where it stopped and simmered. He was there. He was always there.

Dear Heavenly Father…okay! So, the meeting didn't go as planned. But You know that. You also know that I want to scream, to cry, to catch a flight somewhere, anywhere to look for him. Father, I miss him so much. The pain is more than anything I have felt. He has been busy. But now he is missing. No one on earth knows where he is. But You do, Father. Only You. Please, if I can do something, let me know.

She waited. And He responded. *Trust me, Anja. Please.*

She couldn't wait anymore. *Father, I have been trusting You. That is what keeps me going. You have given me the strength to keep going. You are enough. More than enough, really. I wouldn't be here without You. But I need You more than I have before.*

I love you. She coughed, but not from the salty air, from the tears that flooded her nasal passages. The truth rang through her soul. Even when she tried to leave Him, He loved her. More than SJ did. More than SJ ever would. And she was okay with that. It was the only way she would have it.

I love You too, Father. But she couldn't shake it. *So, here's the thing, Daddy, I know that You have a plan, that You have a purpose, a reason for all that You do. So, why did I go the marine base? Why did You lead me there? I got nowhere. Master Sergeant Beck wouldn't tell me anything.* She slowly started to nod as her mouth opened a sliver. *But now I know that he really doesn't know where SJ is. And…he doesn't know where his team is either.* It hit her like the handle of a shovel would if she stepped on the blade.

There were other families who were suffering just like her. There were other people who needed Him just as much, or more, than she did. He needed her to be His hands. She let out a small exclamation!

Father, I am Yours! I am here! Thank You for showing me that I need to be Your hands, that You need me, just like I need You. She paused, realization dawning. *And thank You that SJ has been working hard to bring others to You. Please continue to bless that marine who welcomed me in the gates.*

Don't forget that I have plans for you, Anja. Plans that will be beyond what you can imagine.

I know. I really do. I mean, You brought me SJ. You led us to each other. You did that, and everything else. She sniffled. *And I don't think You would bring us together just to tear us apart. But I am not in charge. You are. And while perfect timing and balancing everyone's lives is Your problem, SJ is my problem too. My complicated, adorable, perfect-for-me-problem. So, please, don't leave me. Stay with me and give me the strength and the patience to wait on You, to wait for SJ to come home. Because he will come home.*

She didn't want it to sound forceful. She wanted it to sound faithful, but she wasn't sure how much faith was behind those words. She only hoped He could truly measure her faith, especially the faith she couldn't see, the faith she couldn't recognize as she tried her best not to crumble and become a part of the sand beneath her feet.

19

The Reunion

"Richardson! Let's move!" It was the nineteenth day overseas and the fifth underground bunker within fifty miles of the team's last known location. The raid would have happened sooner, but their men were sparse, so they called Kyle back, Kyle and his team.

"On three, sir!" Kyle was communicating with his commanding officer, Sergeant Ashby. Kyle stood on the east end of the bunker leading a group of three men while Ashby was stationed on the west side of the bunker accompanied by the three remaining men on the team. Kyle shifted his rifle into his left hand, flattened his right hand, aiming his fingers toward the black sky and quickly twisting his wrist ninety degrees twice. With M16 A4 rifles aimed at unseen targets and goggles that aided them to see in the dark, they squatted, waiting until Kyle opened the door, knowing that the perfect silence would be penetrated within seconds.

Kyle gripped the slab of concrete that served as the door and pulled until the veins in his arms and head started to play peekaboo. Kyle was able to shove the cement door a few inches before Lance Corporal Raymond Jones stood by his side to finish opening the door. Praying that all was well on the other side, they moved in, one right behind the other, rifles aimed, ears alert, eyes engaged.

Despite everything going on, they could smell it. It was stronger than anything else. Ignoring the red stains along the walls and the burgundy substance running down the drains, they moved forward.

Casings littered the concrete floor as they didn't even stop to breathe. Down the first hallway to another hallway that only allowed them to go right or left, Kyle and Jones headed left while Frost and Lee went to the right.

Rifles still igniting a sound they all wished they never had to hear again, they moved on. Doorway after doorway. They whipped to the right and to the left, only pulling the death switch when someone mirrored their actions.

Kyle and Jones got to the fifth door, but it wouldn't budge. There was a single window near the top in the middle of the door, the only one with a window so far. Kyle held up his fingers, first his index, then his middle, then his ring. Simultaneously, they leaned back and shot out their right legs, hitting the door with enough force to burst it wide open. A single figure laid against the far wall. He wasn't chained. But he wasn't moving either. His skin was naturally dark, but they could smell the layers of sweat, dirt, blood, and burning skin. No one else was in the room, so Jones stayed near the door to make sure it stayed that way.

"Marine! Marine!" He gently checked his brother's pulse. It was there. Barely.

Kyle knew there was only one way that the marine was getting out of there. And it meant they had one less gun on their side.

On the other side of the bunker, Ashby, Vince, Isles, and Shaklee were knocking down the tenth door. So far, they only found empty rooms, or human remains. But what mattered then was finding their brothers. The ones they had to believe were still alive.

But there was still nothing.

"Richardson! Report!"

"We found one, sir. Not good. Been held up here watching him. I'm with Jones. Frost and Lee went south."

"Okay, headed that way. Stay put!" Ashby led his group of three around the last corner. A few of them fell. Never to get up again. And for what?

Faced with a hallway that seemed to go on forever, they halted momentarily, taking it in. From left to right, their scanners showed that limp, lifeless bodies plagued the hallway. Two figures were headed their way, weapons aimed at them, but not for long. The third bedroom on their right had at least six men.

"Frost! Lee!" Ashby had to know.

"At your 12, sir!" They said it in unison, despite their years apart from each other. Jones poked his head out of the room with three live images. He gave them a thumbs up, but before he could retreat, Ashby gestured toward the neighboring room at their nine o'clock. Jones nodded, disappeared into the room for less than two seconds, and then joined his team in the hallway outside the only other door with a window. Ashby and Jones kicked it down, causing a ripple of groans as they stormed through the doorway.

Seven men lay scattered at odd, floppy angles. But they were all breathing. One of them wobbly stood to greet them while holding onto the arm of another as he balanced on one leg.

"Brothers!" The first man's name tag read Deeks. His handshake was weak.

"You have no idea how good it is to see you." This soldier's smile was weak, but it was there. His name tag read Gensicki. As Kyle's team helped the rest of the team up and called for their ride home, more name tags became visible. True, they faced the floor as the shirts hung loosely around their bodies, but they could still be read. Munoz. Day. Wheeler. Bates. Brooklyn.

"Let's go home!" Arm in arm, brothers escorted brothers out of the prison, down the hall, and into the light.

I know it was dark because the sun had not yet shown its face. But there was a light only they could see, a light they would never forget.

Kyle, with Phillipe in his arms, brought up the rear. As he neared the cluster of brothers trudging through the green fortress, he sensed something. Not danger. It was something else. Like he needed to find someone. As he sifted through the men, he found him, the man he was looking for, the man God needed him to find.

"SJ?" SJ would have whipped around if he could, but all he could manage was a slow rotation as his grip around Ashby's neck loosened.

"Uh…yeah?" Kyle couldn't see the confusion that clearly, but he could certainly hear it.

"Hi! My name is Kyle Richardson! I am a friend of Anja's!" Before SJ could react, he continued, "Don't worry, man! Just friends. I met her through my wife. We are in the same ward, man! It is so good to see you. Once I heard what the mission was, I prayed I would find you." He took a second to let SJ register all of it, or at least try to. "Anja's been waiting for you, man." He could have said so much more. How Anja prayed for SJ every time she was over at their house. How she loved Jake but wanted SJ more. How she was one of the strongest women he had ever met. But SJ probably already knew. There was only one way to make sure they held each other again. "I just thought you would like to know."

He couldn't see the tears, but he knew they were there. Taking a deep breath, he tried to fight his own. He was right where he needed to be with whom he needed to be with. Thanks to Him. He may have been the only one whose ears picked up on SJ's utterance, but it was unmistakable and truer than anything, "God is so good, man."

Fifty paces later, they approached the CH-53D Sea Stallion. The roar was loud, but it was a comfort from the ringing in their ears that wouldn't leave for at least a few days.

Kyle secured Phillipe in a seat and then went back to the low-ered door as he assisted more brothers to safety. Once everyone was strapped in, including himself, the helicopter started to lift off. He would get these men home. He had no doubt. The only thing that concerned him as he laid his head back for the flight home was the lack of figures he and his team had shot. It was almost abandoned. And that didn't just happen.

20

The Glue

All she could think about was how she had made it to that point.

On her twenty-minute drive back from the beach with Jake in the passenger seat lolling his tongue out the open window, she did a lot of thinking. Well, a lot more thinking. SJ was her problem and would be for eternity. She didn't want it any other way, but at the same time, she could only worry about him so much. And she did too much. She said she would give him to the Lord, trust him with the Lord. And she had tried. But she thought she failed. So it was time.

SJ was in perfect hands and had been even before they met. So, she would still worry about him, but she would worry about him with Him. She wanted to worry, for it was a way she held onto him, but she wasn't going to go crazy looking for him. God knew where SJ was, and that was all she needed to know. Master Sergeant Bates said they had a team looking for SJ and his team. So, she did what she could do, what she could control.

She evaluated what she wanted to accomplish in life. Many people call it a bucket list, but she likes to call it a "becoming list," a list in her brain she can refer to that only gets added to if it is something that she feels will help her to become who He knows she can be, who she wants to become. True, some items on the list required SJ, like going on a service mission trip abroad, eating at a fancy restaurant along the coast and then walking along the beach as they try to push each other into the salty, cold water, and one day having children of their own, but there was one thing that a part of her wanted to do. Would it be easier with SJ? Yes! But she knew this was something she needed to do on her own with Him as a guide. Even if most of her rejected the idea, she heard the cry deep from within. That was what brought her here.

It was a six-hour drive, but it was worth it. They deserved more than she had given them. So today would be the start of a new beginning with her parents.

Father in heaven, I love You so much. Thank You for reminding me to cheerfully do what I can control and to let go of what I cannot. You are in control. And that is what is best for me, SJ, Rebecca, and my parents. Please give me the courage to say what I need to say. Thank You. In the name of Jesus Christ, amen.

Kneeling at the headstones of her parents, she started to talk to them. Yes, they had died, but she knew they were there listening.

"I'm sorry, Daddy, Mommy. For going to such a dark place that I thought I couldn't come back. You didn't raise me that way, and I want you to know that it is not your fault. I want to thank you for raising me the way you did, for teaching me about God, for wanting to go to dinner with me that night.

"I'm sorry I lost you. I'm sorry I was so determined to take care of that itch that it cost you your lives. I'm sorry for being selfish, for being so consumed with me, my wants and my needs, that I forgot about everyone else. You taught me better. You really did. So please never doubt your roles as my parents. You were there for me, even after you died.

"God taught me to stop placing blame on myself. It wasn't getting me anywhere, not anywhere good, anyway. But I want to apologize again, for it was my responsibility. You were my responsibility that night, and I lost that privilege when I lost you. Don't worry, I am truly at peace with it, but that doesn't mean the pain and the sorrow goes away. I feel it every day, but I am learning that it doesn't have to control me. I don't want fear and pain to control me.

"I am more than that because I am His daughter. Just like you promised. Anyway, I am here to let go. I need to..." They hit her before she was ready. The sobs escaped with no way to hold them back. Saying it out loud was much different than keeping it inside her heart. She bent over further, feeling the weight grow heavier. She couldn't do this. She couldn't let them go. And she definitely couldn't forgive herself. There was no way to change the past. What she did was unforgiveable. The worst part was that she brought it on herself.

Father in heaven, I need You. She doesn't know where it came from, but she heard the prayer escape her lips.

She was still the only one in the cemetery. Still alone. But there was no mistaking it. Someone knelt beside her and cried with her. She heard her soft weeps. Another came over and enfolded them in his arms. She tried to see them, to really open her eyes, but still no one was there, not that she could see. So, she closed her eyes, and she let Him in.

Father in heaven, thank You for bringing me closer to You, to my parents. Thank You for letting me be an instrument in Your hands. Thank You for showing me that You are in everything, in all of the details, that You know me more than I know myself. Thank You for the peace, the overwhelming joy I feel inside of me as I continue on the path You have set for me. I love you, Daddy. I really do. In the name of Jesus Christ, amen.

Opening her eyes, she looked once again at the headstones that bore her parents' names: James Brackett Whittle and Reva Evangeline Whittle. She took a deep breath. "I need to let go. I cannot hold onto the past. I have to move forward. He wants me to." Her voice grew quieter. "And I want to. I need to let you go to Him. I will be with you again soon. Don't worry. I will never forget you. You will always be a part of me, but I don't want to take you away from Him, so please, tell Him I love Him. And please send my love to Ray. I love you too, Mommy and Daddy. Never forget that."

Just before she placed her keys in the ignition, she picked up her phone she had left in the truck. The display on her phone informed her that she had ten missed calls, three from Master Sergeant Bates and seven from Rebecca. Torn between who to call, she chose to call the man who held her future in his hands.

21

The Future

*S*he was there in a heartbeat.

Sprinting through the halls, she passed at least twenty-one crying strangers, and yet, in those fleeting moments, she couldn't help but feel close to them. The lady at the front desk told her to go down the hall to the elevator, up to the third floor, left toward the window, then right once she got to the window, and through the doors. He should be there. Somewhere. How she remembered those instructions escapes her.

He was more handsome than ever. She thought it was because he always looked good in his uniform, no matter that his uniform was varying shades of brown. It highlighted his hair. But more importantly, it spotlighted his eyes with an intensity she didn't see otherwise. Like he was on a mission. Like there was nothing that would stop him from doing what he needed to do. Like it was him, his team, and his God.

She knew why: he looked more handsome than ever because he was there. He was real. She could reach out, fold the fabric of his uniform in her hands. She could lift her eyes and admire all of him as she gazed into his chocolate eyes. She could smell the dirt that refused to ever go away, even when they first met. She could taste the water he just drank as she brought her lips to his. She could hear the rumble in his throat as he spoke directly into her ear, "I love you, sunshine."

It was quiet, but there couldn't have been more power behind those words.

He held onto her and she let him. He owed her four weeks' worth of love, hugs, cuddles, walks, cries, talks, laughs, all of it. And he knew she was going to hold him to it.

Without letting go, she had to make sure he understood, "Do you know what you did?"

"I do." She felt a tear softly dance with strands of her hair as it landed on her scalp like a raindrop falling through trees in a jungle.

She knew he wouldn't say it, so she reminded him. "You brought them home, Ray. You brought them home." She repeated it, letting it sink into his soul, letting it sink into her soul. It rested on her heart, and she knew that even if he was away from her, she had a family. She had him. All he wanted to do was make sure that other families got what they deserved: that they would be together, just like she and Kyle were. God had a purpose for sending him away. Not only for other loved ones that the Lord treasures. It was for them too. He didn't do it to rip him from her so that limitation could constrict them. It was to liberate both of them.

She could see that he let her words resonate within him as they floated and settled inside his heart. He brought them home. He and his team brought families home. All thanks to Him for calling them back, for trusting them to be willing to do His work, His will, no matter what. He needed them, and they accepted the call.

"Sunshine... I need to ask you something." Moments had passed, and the only movement was his lips as he caught her breath and kissed her ear.

"Ray, I can't—"

"Don't worry, baby. I'm right here." He squeezed her a little tighter. "And I'm not going anywhere." No matter how much she wanted to believe him, she knew it could be different tomorrow. With him, she never knew.

"Okay." She hoped he heard the truth that rang in her words.

"How are you doing?" She pulled back, ever so slightly. Her arms were still around his neck while her legs held onto his waist.

"What?" Her eyebrows angled toward her nose as her head tilted to the side. He just laughed and repeated the same question. Her eyebrows relaxed as he brought his lips to her forehead.

"How about we head out and talk about it?" He directed her toward the exit.

"Okay." She stepped back. "Wait! Really?"

She followed his lead and reached for his hand.

"Yes! I just need to notify Sergeant Ashby." She squeezed his hand and then watched him walk away from her just like he had the day they took him. But He brought him back. They were together. No matter how many times he had to walk away from her, she knew he would always come back.

After checking with Sergeant Ashby, Kyle walked back toward Kate, grabbed her hand, interlaced his fingers with hers, and escorted her out the doors, past the glass wall, down the hall, down the elevators, down another hall, and out the automatic front door of the hospital. Once they got to her Kia van, he held open the door for her as she jumped into the passenger seat. He then walked around the front of the tan hunk of machine and hopped into the driver's seat. She handed him the keys, but he placed them in the cup holder in between their seats.

"We need to do something first." She didn't care that they were sitting in the concrete parking garage.

"You name it!" He extended his hands and her hands found his. He bowed his head, and she mirrored him.

"Dear Heavenly Father, we want to take a much-needed moment to thank You. Thank You that we are together. Thank You that we are a team. Thank You for the love that Kate and I share, for the love that we will continue to share and that will grow with time and experience. Thank You," he paused, "for helping me and my team save more of Your children. Thank You for letting me be an instrument in Your hands. And thank You for always protecting Kate, especially when I am not here. Thank You for loving us more than we know. Thank You for everything, Father. We love You. In the name of Jesus Christ, amen."

"And thank *you*." There was no explanation needed.

"So…" He clapped his hands, clutched the keys, chucked them in the air, caught them, and delivered them to the ignition. "Where to, my sunshine?"

She lifted her index finger to her chin and tapped. "Let's go home!" He was hoping she would say that.

An hour later, he pulled the van into the driveway. After putting it into park, dropping off the keys in the bowl on top of the entry table, and taking their shoes off, they found their way to the bedroom.

Still in his uniform and her in her purple V-neck and black sweatpants, they flopped on the bed. His arms rested above his head, but he turned his head to look at her. The way her subtle red hair spread out around her head like a lion's mane. The way her blue eyes danced with his when she turned her head toward him. The way he just wanted to reach out and bop her adorable nose. The way her lips held onto words that she wanted to share.

"What is it, sunshine?" Her white teeth showed and he couldn't help but giggle as he looked at her two front crooked teeth. She had refused braces when she was younger, but he didn't care. She was as close to perfect as anyone could be.

"I have news for you!" She pushed off the bed as she turned to rest her head against her left wrist. "Anja and I started a support group. A lot of us have husbands in the marines, but some of us don't. We are just hurting. Hurt comes in various forms, and we don't want to turn anyone away. Rebecca has been helping too." Without any more hesitation, she went on, "We have had three meetings so far." Her voice dropped. "It started the week you left." He just listened, a smile still on his face as he watched her. "We cry a lot. That's what happens when you put a lot of sad women together."

They both laughed, Kyle more so because he loved the way her eyes crinkled when she did her happy laugh. "But it is more than just crying. He is there, Ray! He is there every time, every second. We can feel Him. Anja, Rebecca, and I are trying to share Him, His love. That's why we started it, or He did, through Anja. She initiated it, and I wanted to help. It is every Thursday, here, at noon. We take turns providing lunch and we pray, eat, and then talk. And cry, of course. But He is crying with us. I can feel it. He doesn't want us to be sad. He doesn't want us to hurt. That is why He sent His Son. And that is one reason Christ said yes. So we wouldn't have to hurt as much for as long. He loves us so much, Ray. He really does!" Her smile lit up the room. He loved her. Even more so when the passion sang through her words, when her love for Him was truer and louder than anything else.

"I love you." He kept smiling. "You know that, right?" The right side of his mouth lifted ever so slightly higher than the left.

"Yes, I do. With all my heart." She leaned forward and kissed his nose. "Did *you* know that I tolerate you?" Her eyes disappeared as she scrunched up her nose in a fit of laughter. He couldn't resist. He pinched her sides, and another fit of laughter escaped between her teeth. She pushed further into the pillow as he leaned closer to her. "I'm just kidding, my handsome soldier." She placed her hands on both sides of his face. "I am honored to love you, to cherish you, to be a part of you."

He looked her in the eyes and held on. "I will never take you for granted." And then his crooked smile was back. She lifted her head and kissed his cracked lips.

"Good!" She brought her hands up to his neck and easily found his ticklish spot—one of them. He bounced up in a burst of energy.

"Oh, it's on, sunshine!"

22

The Door

No, the drive back home was not stress free. No, it was not all entirely within the legal speed limit. But she knew it would all be worth it. After finding the right exit, she was at his front door in twenty-two minutes. Well, the front doors of the hospital.

"Excuse me! Excuse me!" She raised her hand at a passing nurse. "Do you know where my husband is?"

"What is your husband's name?" She stopped to face Anja.

"SJ! SJ Gensicki!" Looking down at the clipboard in her right arm, she shook her head.

"I'm sorry, ma'am, I don't, but the lady at the front desk should be able to help you." The nurse pointed behind her, and Anja realized she had breezed right past the front desk.

She waved her hand at the nurse as she briskly retraced her steps. "SJ Gensicki! Please?" The nurse, whose name tag read "Brewer," scanned the computer that was slightly hidden on the other side of the counter.

"He is room 252! He is—"

"Thank you!" The nurse just smiled as Anja yelled while running for the elevator. Ignoring that she never wanted to step foot in that hospital again after seeing another life gone, she pushed the button not once, or twice, but at least ten times. She jumped into the elevator and proceeded to poke the level 2 button until the doors closed. Even then, she shifted her weight from her right leg to her left leg, grateful no one else was in the elevator. Not that she would have cared anyway.

Seconds later, she was out the doors that hadn't even opened all the way. Finding the hallway that wound past a wall of glass, she turned right and was faced with another set of doors. That still didn't stop her.

She could hear him calling her, praying for her, asking for her. And she was finally there. He didn't need to worry anymore.

Through the doors, she burst to find another desk. But there was something else that caught her attention. Actually, three some-things—three numbers, 2, 5, 2.

He was just behind that closed door.

But she was tired of closed doors. And this one she could open. So she did.

She ignored the nurses, gesturing toward her, asking questions she didn't hear. Because he was there, and she was there in the same room. After three years and eight months, they were together. No matter that it was the fourth of July. This was better than any holiday she had ever experienced.

But she had to stop. This was just a dream. Doubt filled her soul. There was no way this was happening. It had been too long. He was missing in action. No one knew where he was except God. And she was okay with that. He was in perfect hands. He always had been. And he always would be. She accepted that. She was okay. True, she cried every day and even harder during the support group meetings, but she had a right to, a reason to.

But it could be possible, right? Anything was possible with God. She would recognize that curly blonde hair anywhere even if it was still caked in dirt and other stuff she refused to think about, even if the last time she saw him, the curls were gone. But other guys had blonde, curly hair, a pointy nose, and a defined jawline like his. The man on the bed had a highly defined jawline she almost didn't recognize. Even underneath the blanket, she could almost point out every rib, the outline of one kneecap. She couldn't help but shudder.

It wasn't until she finally saw them. They had been staring at her the moment she stepped into the room. Well, the moment she burst into the room.

Emeralds. They stared right at her, right through her, right into her. And she let them. Until she ran out of the room.

"Father!" She let her shortest prayer escape as she left the way she came, to the elevators, down a level, and right back out the front doors. The park was only a block away, and she wouldn't argue with a little exercise. All she could think about was him or what she had to believe was him.

It wasn't just the weight loss or the hair or the smile or the missing leg. There was something else, something deeper that she saw but didn't recognize. It was him. There was no mistaking it, but the man lying in that bed was not the same one she watched walk away from her all those years ago. And she couldn't face it.

After finding a secluded tree in the park, she slumped against the trunk and screamed.

Father, I did not sign up for this. I don't remember this part of the deal. You gave him to me. You trusted him with me. And I trusted him with You. I agreed to let him go serve his country, to serve You. And he did that. And now he is back. But, Daddy, You took him from me! Why would You do that? Where is he? I know that that is his body, but the light in his eyes isn't there. Not the way it used to be. We had a deal. I gave him to You, and You would take care of him. But You didn't, Daddy! Why didn't You take care of him like You promised? Any response would have been drowned out by the flood of gasps and tears that came next.

I wanted so badly to hold her close. So I did. And I squeezed. Her breathing calmed the longer I held on. And I never let go, not even after she opened her eyes, not even as she watched a couple, hand in hand, walk through the park, not even as she wished that things would go back to the way they were before the war, before he left, before he asked her to give up everything.

She thought she could do it, but she was beginning to think that she couldn't, that she didn't have anything more to give. She had given it all. And for what? For a stranger to come home and claim to be her husband?

For several minutes, she sat there, watching, waiting, listening.

Her phone continued to ring. And she continued to ignore it. But she couldn't anymore, not after what she saw. It was a picture of

SJ. Well, the selfie had been taken by her, so both of them were in it. She zoomed up on his face. He had always been a tease when it came to taking pictures. He never would behave himself. But he did for that picture. It wasn't planned, wasn't posed for. She just happened to capture it at the perfect time. She had been looking at the camera, like she was supposed to. But he was looking at her, the way only he could, just like he had when he saw her in the hospital room. But she had ignored it. No, she had run from it. She had run from him.

On her sprint back to him, she made notes, *Daddy, I am so sorry for everything, including how I handled that situation, my anger at You, at the situation. I keep saying that I trust You, and then I go and do something like this. I am so sorry. I really will try to stop doubting You, to fully and truly trust You. I am here, and he is here. I owe You everything. The light may be dim, but at least, You are still in him. I see that now. It was just a lot to take in. I am sorry, Daddy. No more running. Not from You, and not from SJ.* She couldn't help but chuckle at the irony. *I love you, Daddy. In the name of Jesus Christ, amen.*

There was nothing slow about this entry. She leaped to his bedside but stopped just shy of the armrest. With an apology in her eyes, she couldn't get a word out.

"Hello, my love!" It was as if nothing had happened. There was more energy in his voice than in his body. It was him. There was no doubt. Not anymore. Not ever again. Giving up on holding back, she maneuvered around the railing and planted her lips on his forehead.

"Hi, my prince!"

"I'm home." He looked up and found himself lost in his own ocean. It was real. She was there with him, where he wanted her to stay for eternity. He patted the empty spot next to him. She swung her legs up to settle right next to him. But all she felt was bone.

She couldn't just ignore it, though; he wasn't the same man that had left her all those years ago.

"It's okay, love." It was just the two of them. She heard him chuckle as she ever so gently rested her head on his shoulder, or what was left of it. "I'm okay. Remember?" It was barely a whisper, but the words were just for her.

"I do." She smiled as she angled her head so she could see those eyes again, so she could remember what home looked like, what it felt like. That was when he lifted his head less than two inches just to kiss her forehead before his head fell back against the pillow, and then again to kiss her hair that always smelled like coconut, and then again on the part down the center of her head, and then once more in between her eyes as she lifted her head toward him.

He couldn't resist. He pinched her nose. Her giggle sent his heart soaring; he was afraid he wouldn't be able to catch it.

After pulling back, she smiled bigger than she had in three years and eight months and kissed his lips once again.

"I love you, Scott James Gensicki."

"Oh, the full name comes out!" He chuckled, his head again resting on the pillow. "I love you more, Anja Rose Gensicki!"

"I'll let you win…this time!" She bit her lip as she waited for him to tease her back.

"Oh, I won the second I met you." His lips didn't rise as high as he wanted them to, but she saw the smile travel through his eyes and enfold both of them. She wouldn't admit it out loud, but he won!

"So, what's new with you?" She wanted to make light of the situation, at least for now. If it sunk in at all like it had earlier, she didn't know if she could handle it. She may be strong, but she didn't think she was that strong.

"The usual: dehydration, starvation, lack of nutrients, an amputated leg, a weakened heart. At least until you broke down the door."

"Oh, sounds like you've had quite the eventful adventure!" He joined her in laughter. But she cut hers short.

"Love, what's wrong?" He tried to sit up but couldn't. "I thought we were being funny!" She just shook her head before she was able to speak.

"I just have been waiting for this…for so long, and now that it is here, now that you are here"—she cupped the left side of his face with her right hand—"I am whole. I've just been waiting so long to see you, to hold you, to hear you, to have you."

His lips curled together a bit as his face grew sympathetic. "You have always had me. All of me." She smiled as he wiped the tear from her cheek.

"I know."

"Besides, you can admit that you missed me." His eyebrows showed that he was teasing her.

"Well, I did miss your laugh!"

"I knew it!" He leaned his forehead to rest against hers. "I really missed you, Anja." He choked on his words as each one came out with a struggle.

"I really missed you, SJ." She held his head in her hands as their foreheads nuzzled each other. And she just breathed, with him.

After several moments, he asked, "So, how is my dad?" His tone was upbeat. Until she clenched her teeth and looked away. "Anja." With all the energy he had, he used his right hand to touch her chin as he also tried to hide the fear that just invaded his whole soul. "What's wrong?"

23

The Baby

The one place where she never wanted to set foot again. Not after what happened only twenty-three weeks prior. She promised herself that she wouldn't do it again, that she would never need to again. But God had other plans. So there she was, in a hospital room, her life on the line, even though he was hooked up to the machines. He was the one with a bandage on his head. He was the one with the missing right leg.

She had said no. No, he could not go serve in the military. Not that it was up to her really. But she still said no. No, she would not let him go. Not then. Not ever. Especially not now. But without fully realizing it, she had also said no to truly, fully living her life, to letting go, to trusting the Lord with every single part of her, to receiving answers to yet more questions, questions only He could answer. Though He never seemed to answer those questions.

"SJ," she paused as she choked on sobs and squeezed the hand she had not released since she was allowed to be in the same room as him, "I am here, baby. Ever since you were born. And always."

It had been that way ever since March 9, 1993, just a little over twenty-six years prior. He had been in her arms for the first time after nine long months. She was a new mother. Her first shot at being what she had dreamed of being since as long as she could remember. After years of no results and lots of prayers, the Lord said yes and had sent her and Johnny a son.

Johnny walked in the red front door.

"I'm home!" But she didn't come. "Hey, Becky! I'm home!" She had done this once before, made him play hide-and-seek when he got home, but that was after they first got married. She hadn't done it in years, and yet he was ready. He had learned that with her, he never knew what came next. So, to living room. She wasn't there. Not even behind couches. Starting to become impressed that a nine-month pregnant lady could hide so well, he moved toward the kitchen.

He couldn't help but laugh. "You are impossible!" She stood up as straight as she could while slowly scooting the trash can behind her body. Her mouth was full, so she couldn't smile all the way, but the whole story was laid out before him. "You realize that I am the one who takes the trash out, right? So I can see the donut boxes that you try so hard to hide." He took a few steps toward her as she swallowed the last donut, her twelfth donut that afternoon. "I just wonder why you don't ever save me one!" He reached her and wrapped his arms around her body, having to stand a few inches further away from her than usual.

"You know I try! I just can't! They are so delicious!" Tears started to surface. "So yummy! I'm sorry." She rested her head against his chest and cried. This was starting to become normal. She would get really passionate about something and then cry. The other day, he walked home to her crying because of a McDonald's commercial. He had to walk away so as to not show her that he was laughing and rolling his eyes, quite a bit.

He placed his hand on the back of her head and started to play with her hair. "You just owe me dozens and dozens and dozens of donuts...after the baby is born." She lifted her head to look into his green eyes. "Although, I am more concerned about all of the donuts we will have to get him." He pointed at the beautiful lump. They started to laugh. She loved him even more in that moment. He always could make her laugh. Even if she felt like crying, which she had for the majority of the past nine months.

"How about we celebrate his birth with donuts? And his first birthday, and every birthday after that!" She would have jumped up and down if she could.

"How about we see if you still like donuts after he is born?" Her face changed in an instant. It was a look he didn't recognize. "Becky? What's wrong?"

"Uh… Johnny…" Finally, her jaw returned to a normal position, but it was still not functioning properly.

"Yes?" He placed his hands on her shoulders and leaned down to look right into her blue-green eyes. "What do you need? I'm right here!"

"I need you to get the car!" The twinkle was back in her eyes.

"He's coming?" Anja nodded! "He's coming!" He bounced away from her as he grabbed the key chain off the wall by the front door and grabbed her go-bag from the closet just on the other side of the front door. Then, bag over his shoulder and keys in his hands, he went back to the kitchen and escorted her to the front door, through it, under the darkening sky, to the car that he left in the roundabout driveway.

After several minutes of Johnny asking so many questions while Becky was worrying about the water they just left on the hardwood kitchen floor, they made it to the hospital.

"Hello, Mrs. Gensicki. It's good to see you are back!" Dr. Peterson timed his walk through that hall perfectly. He had been their doctor throughout the entire nine months. And now he was going to be there for the finale beginning. After checking her in and getting her settled on the bed, he asked, "How would you like to do it today? You still have time for an epidural." She looked at Johnny first. But he just shrugged.

"That's up to you, baby." She looked back at Dr. Peterson.

"I'll do an epidural." She hadn't been afraid of needles. But she was tempted to change that once she saw the size of the needle the doctor was about to shove into her back.

He instructed her to shift so her legs could hang off the bed. That way, it would give him a better angle. She did so with Johnny's help and sat as tall as she could. He was poking around and talking to the nurse, but she was looking at Johnny, who was smiling. He stepped closer and grabbed both of her hands.

"Remember, I'm right here, baby." She nodded and bit her lip.

"Okay." She continued to nod. "Okay."

"Hey"—he let her hands drop as he took her face in his hands—"right here. Look at me. You are doing so good, baby. He is coming. Think about how soon you will be able to hold him. We can take him on trips, and I can go on runs with him, and you can teach him how to cook, since we both know I still struggle with that."

"Done!"

Rebecca turned her head. "Wait! Really?"

"Yes!" Dr. Peterson seemed sure, so she wasn't about to worry. With Johnny's help, she was able to sit back against the pillows. "We need to let that settle in, but I am going to check your diameter again." Rebecca laid her head against the pillow.

"Oh, wow! I can feel the medicine kicking in! That feels good. Really good! Hey, baby! You should try this!" He laughed and shook his head.

"I'll pass, baby, but thanks!"

"I tried!" She shrugged and started to close her eyes.

"Hey, Becky! What are you doing?" Johnny placed his hand on her shoulder and leaned over her. But she didn't open her eyes.

"She's a 7! Let's bring this baby home!" Dr. Peterson looked up. "Rebecca?"

"Dr. Peterson, she fell asleep! Why would she fall asleep?" Johnny's voice was louder than intended.

"I am not sure…" The doctor jumped up and slapped the gloves off his hands. "Unless…"

"Unless what?"

"Nurse, I need you to…" He kept speaking, kept giving commands, but Johnny didn't hear them.

Father in heaven, please, more than anything right now, I want her to be okay. Please, Father, please help her be okay. Please keep her here with me. I need her. Please. In the name of Jesus Christ, amen.

The nurse was pumping a clear liquid into Rebecca's IV. "What is that?" He harshly pointed at it.

Dr. Peterson spoke up, "It will help to counteract the epidural I administered. It must have been injected in the wrong spot, sending it up her spinal cord to her heart." His voice dropped an octave.

"That is why she was falling asleep." He didn't need to explain that her heart was falling asleep. He didn't want to hear those words. Instead, he wanted to yell at the doctor, to blame him for threatening his wife's life, to blame him for threatening to take away their baby. But the concerned look on the doctor's face told him that he was doing that to himself.

All he could do was stare at her face, waiting for those beautiful eyes to look at him. But that didn't happen.

"Becky!" He leaned down and kissed her forehead. She looked so peaceful. Free of pain. Free of the waves of emotions that had plagued her for nine months. He almost wanted to let her sleep. But a part of him knew that she wasn't sleeping. She was dying as the epidural told her heart to stop beating.

"*Doctor!*" he yelled—a full-blown yell where spit flew out of his mouth, across the bed his wife was lying in, and landed on the doctor's face. But the line on the monitor only grew more horizontal. Dr. Peterson didn't respond, other than to continue to check Rebecca's vitals.

Father in heaven, please... He didn't finish before she started breathing again.

She took a deep breath in. "What happened?"

"That doesn't matter!" He shook his head as he leaned over her body and wrapped what he could in his arms. "It doesn't matter."

"Baby, what's wrong?" She felt his tears on her green and blue hospital gown.

"Don't worry about it! I'll tell you later!" He couldn't look at Dr. Peterson. "Let's have this baby!" That was when he looked at the doctor, silently making sure they could still have the baby, that he was still alive.

Minutes later, she was in full swing. But he wouldn't come. After ten painful pushes, he still wouldn't come. And Dr. Peterson couldn't explain why.

"He should be coming. He is in the right position. Take a few moments to take deep breaths and then we will keep trying." Rebecca nodded and waved her hand at Johnny.

"Help me?"

"What do you need?"

"I need to sit up a bit more. I can't handle another second in this position. It isn't working." They locked arms as he lifted her to sit up more.

"Let's try this again, shall we?" Dr. Peterson was ready.

She gave one more push, and he came flying out. Literally. There was no stopping him. Luckily, Dr. Peterson was there to catch him.

After the nurse wiped him down and wrapped him in the Winnie the Pooh blanket they bought for him, she handed him to Rebecca. And she saw he had his daddy's eyes.

"Rebecca?"

"Sorry, Dr. Anderson." She couldn't look him in the eyes. She didn't want to see what they weren't telling her.

He was the doctor who told her that her son's leg had to be amputated if he was going to live. He was the one who told her that his body wasn't strong enough to keep going. All she remembered was "your son…can't…breathe…lost his leg…" That is all she needed to know. No, it was more than she wanted to know. Because then she was able to figure out everything that he wasn't telling her. Everything that he wasn't telling Anja either.

Anja said she needed air, but that was an hour ago.

Dear Father, please. Don't take him from me. Don't take him away. You have Johnny. Please don't take SJ too. I need You. In the name of Your Beloved Son, Jesus Christ, amen.

Rebecca, I am right here.

"Really?" She heard Anja's voice. She must have walked in while she was praying. Looking from her to the doctor, she thought it appeared he was taking the tube out, SJ's oxygen tube. "Wait, Dr. Anderson! You can't do…" Rebecca stopped and saw what Anja saw: SJ was breathing without it. After three weeks of using that machine to pump oxygen into her only child, his body was finally ready to do it on its own.

For the first time in several weeks, it finally happened: she felt her heart beat. Steady. *Thump-thump.* Consistent. *Thump-thump.* Rhythmic. *Thump-thump.* Independent. *Thump-thump.* Because so was his.

Father in heaven, thank You. Thank You. She sat back against the chair that had become her place of residence and grasped her son's hand.

Father, please forgive me for doubting You, for disrespecting You. I do trust You. I really do. He is in Your perfect hands. And I am grateful for You and for Your plan. Thank You that Johnny is with you. And SJ is with me. I am Yours. Thank You. In the name of my Savior, Jesus Christ, amen.

"Rebecca!" Dr. Anderson was no longer the only other person in the hospital room. There were two other nurses and a third one she could see running toward his room. A familiar-looking machine rested on the other side of SJ's bed, where Anja was just sitting. It was the machine that pumps electricity into someone whose heart has stopped, into someone who is no longer breathing on his or her own.

All she could do was stare at Anja being carried out of the room that grew further from her as she too was escorted away from her dead son.

24

The War

"Did you hear?" Anja had left to go talk to the doctor about the details of the next steps, and he couldn't stand the awkward silence between him and his mom. They had shed enough tears together already. He just couldn't believe that he was gone.

"What?" She looked up.

"They will discharge me sometime this week and then we can go home since they know I can stand on my own." Less than twenty-four hours seemed like a reasonable and likely timeframe, or so he hoped.

"That's good." Her lips curled up, but it wasn't a smile.

"What's wrong, Mom?" She closed her eyes and kept them that way.

"I've been thinking."

He gave a quick laugh. "I can tell. What's on your mind?" He sat up on his own. He wanted to know, more so because he hadn't heard her voice in too long. He didn't want to play the blame game, so he soaked in every word.

"He sent you to fight. He asked you to go, and you said yes."

There was no doubt when he admitted, "I did."

She shook her head again. "But why?" SJ didn't respond at first. It wouldn't hurt to tell her that he had been wondering the same thing, that he wanted the same answer, but that would lead to a dark place in his heart he wasn't willing to go.

"I don't know the answer to that question, Mom. Only He does." She leaned forward in her chair and stroked his gruffy cheek.

"I know. I just wish He would share that with me, with us." He smiled, knowing that He would if and when it was best for them.

"Me too, Mom. Me too." Then the room grew quiet again, so SJ fell asleep for the fifth time in one day.

There he was. In the same bunker part of him died in. But he couldn't really tell, actually. All he knew was that everything was black. Not even just black, but dark. The darkest he had ever seen. He couldn't see or touch the walls, but he certainly felt them. He knew they were there, close by, lurking, waiting.

He couldn't stay there for long. He had to get out. But he had already tried. He even tried to save his friends, so all he could do now was wait until someone rescued him, until someone came to find him.

But there wasn't enough time. It was getting closer—all of it, the darkness, the invisible walls, the fear.

He couldn't let it in. He wouldn't let it in. So off he went, one foot in front of the other, closer to anything but that, closer to what he hoped would be light—freedom, joy, God. Was He there? He couldn't be! He didn't live in this, this filth, this prison. He was the Master, the Creator of freedom, of life. There was no way He was there.

But He had to be. He said He would be. No matter what. But He wasn't. He was nowhere to be seen.

And then he heard what he had heard for what felt like four years too long: the sound of gunshots. All from him. None from his team. But he didn't have a gun. He wasn't holding anything, not physically anyway.

And then he detected another sound, one of something dropping, falling. And he knew that sound too. The soulless bodies were piling up in front of him, next to him, behind him.

He closed his eyes and did the only thing he could think to do. "Father!" And then he felt it. He was there. He couldn't see Him, but there was no mistaking that He was there.

"Stop fighting, My son."

"What do You mean?" But there was no response. He waved his hands around, hoping to touch Him, to reach Him. But there was no one there.

"Look, My son." So SJ opened his eyes, but the bodies were closer. There was blood everywhere, and the faces looked familiar because they were the faces of the figures that he had killed, the faces of the figures whose hearts stopped all because he pulled the trigger.

"Father, that isn't helping. Please, help me! Help me get out of here!"

"I need you to look, SJ. Just *look*." He was. He was trying, but he no longer wanted to look. It was just taking him deeper into himself, to a place he hid from everyone, even God.

Look! Look! He repeated it in his head time and time again, hoping that would help him understand what He wanted from him.

"Father, all I want is You. I am trying to look, but what I see isn't what I want. I want to see You. I can't handle this. There is too much darkness." He choked on a sob before he added, "It isn't just around me, Dad. I can see it inside me. It is tainting my soul. I am not worthy of You, of Your plan, but I want You anyway. I need You, Dad. Please, please I just want You." He dropped to his knees on the stone-cold surface.

"I am right here, My son. I always have been." And then he saw it.

"SJ?" He knew that voice. It was his favorite one. It was the one he fell asleep listening to, the one he dreamed of hearing again someday. There it was again. It sounded close, like it was right next to him.

"Anja?" And just like that, his dream was gone.

"Yes!" He heard her relief. "Hi, love! Hi! How are you? Are you okay? Does anything hurt?"

"Uh…no." He squeezed his eyes, willing himself to wake up.

"Tell me what's wrong, love! Please." He felt a forceful sensation in his left hand.

"Nothing, princess, nothing." He was almost there.

"You just said that you weren't okay." He laughed.

"You asked me several questions. I just answered the one I remembered."

"Okay! Okay, love. Okay." He saw her, those eyes, that hair, those cheeks, that nose. And he remembered how much he had missed her, all of her, every single part of her.

"It's okay, love." He tried to sound convincing. "I'm okay." And she did something he wasn't prepared for. She smiled.

"I know."

"You do, do you?" She gave a sharp nod and sat straighter.

"I do, indeed." He couldn't help but love her more. He knew that there was no doubt in her mind that she knew. What? He didn't know. But she did.

"And what do you know?" He angled his head from one side to the other as sharply as he could, trying to give the sass right back to her.

"I know that you are okay. I know that you will be okay. No matter what, you are in His hands. You always have been."

All he could do was stare at her, grasping for a faith like hers because he didn't know where his had gone. It was still there. But not like it used to be. Once he thought about it, he knew it was wavering. He just didn't know how to face it.

"Okay," he said it with confidence. He knew she was right, even though he didn't feel it.

She released his hand, lifted out of her chair, and lied on the bed next to him. He wanted it to be like this forever.

He woke up two hours later.

"Hi, Mom," he tried to whisper, not that it was that hard. But he didn't want to wake his beautiful sleeping wife, who was curled underneath his chin.

"Hi, honey." She gave him a small smile. "How are you feeling?"

"Good." He returned her smile, but his was a tad bigger. "Much better now. How are you?"

"I'm hangin' in there." He opened his right hand, and her hand found his.

"Don't worry, Mom. Everything will be okay. We have to remember that." She nodded and closed her eyes.

"I know. I know." She opened her eyes. "I need to be more grateful you are here." The tears started coming. "You are home."

"And I'm here to stay." He meant it with all that he had. She squeezed her baby boy's hand.

"So, when are you going to give me grandbabies?" He couldn't help but laugh. Yes, it was funny, but even more so, they needed the break in conversation. He just wasn't quite expecting that subject.

"When we are ready!"

A weary voice chimed in, "We wanted to wait for him to come home so our baby could be raised by both of us." She wiggled her head as she buried herself farther into his neck and brought her arms closer to her chest.

"So, you are saying that I will have a grandbaby soon?" SJ melted as he felt her laughter on his neck. And then he felt her lips on his neck. He wrapped his arms around her and squeezed. He held onto her, onto the memory, because knowing her, that was probably the best sleep she had had in years. The same goes for him.

In that moment, Dr. Anderson popped back in and rattled a few notes off to them. "So, what are you saying?" Anja, still on the bed next to SJ where she had been for most of the past few weeks while SJ was completing therapy, looked at Dr. Anderson, hope escaping from her eyes.

No, his muscles weren't as prominent, but they would be back soon enough. He was sure of it. When she grazed his stomach as she wrapped her arms around his waist, she didn't reach as many ribs. As she lifted her head to look at the doctor, she grazed SJ's cheek. The flesh on his colored cheek. Her other hand played with his hair, massaging his scalp and tangling his long, curly hair. She had finally washed it. He said he didn't mind the grungy look of his hair, but she did, so he let her wash it.

"He can go home tomorrow. You can all go home tomorrow." SJ chuckled as the doctor added, "And take showers."

"Yes, sir!"

He heard Anja whisper, "I love you." And he couldn't wait to be home with her, just him and her.

25

The Beginning

It was like a dream. The sunlight was streaming through the window just perfectly. It was like God was sending them a special gift, a hint at a bright future.

His head folded into the white pillow beneath. His curly hair brushed against his forehead, but his eyes were free of its reach. His long brown eyelashes cast a shadow at the peak of his full cheek. His nose pointed toward the sky as the sound of a dying moose escaped his pink parted lips. His white teeth served as a whistle.

He was perfect. Even the perfect snorer. She had missed that more than she realized as she lifted her hand and started tracing shapes on his shirt. First, she signed her name and then his name and then his promise. It was the promise he made to her the day she poured out her heart to him: "I, Scott James Gensicki, promise you, Anja Rose, that while I will always run to God first…"

"I will always make sure you are running with me." He finished it for her with a gentle whisper, and it made her weak. She hadn't heard those words since he first uttered them all those years ago, but he remembered every word.

"Good morning, handsome." Just then, Jake sprung up at the end of the bed and rushed to them. In a matter of seconds, he had managed to wedge himself in between them. He gave SJ a few kisses on the face and then looked at Anja. He only gave SJ kisses, rarely her, not even before SJ got home twenty-five weeks ago.

Their laughter filled the room, as did Jake's excited bark, until his barking faded away as he jumped off the bed and disappeared.

"Duty calls!" He threw off the white duvet as he slipped one flesh foot and one prosthetic foot into his slippers as he too vanished down the hall. She turned over and submerged her forehead into her white pillow.

Father, thank You. Thank You. Thank You. He has been home for six months, and he is still home. They officially released him from duty just yesterday, so he is here for good. He is home to stay, and he is doing really well with his new leg. He gets better with it each day. The therapy really helped. Thank You. I love you, Daddy. In the name of Jesus Christ, amen.

Her peaceful moment didn't last long before she found herself racing her stomach. She wiped her mouth, brushed her teeth, and folded herself in her periwinkle-blue and off-white polka dot robe.

She walked out of the bathroom to their adjoining master bedroom. The king bed was to her left in the middle of the gold and white-striped wall. Two nightstands guarded each side of the head of the bed. A cream bench with curly wooden legs rested at the end of the bed. To its right was the white door that led to her dream walk-in closet. She only started filling it once he got back.

What struck her as odd, though, was that SJ was sitting on one of the chairs just on the other side of the French doors on the patio. She crept her way closer to him.

"I just can't get over it: that dream keeps coming back. I haven't even told Anja yet, but I had it again last night. The only thing that keeps me sane is her. It's always been her, but I need to tell her. It's part of me now. Please, please give me the strength to tell her. In the name of Jesus Christ, amen." She turned the handle and gently put her weight against the door. Silently, it opened, and she stepped out into the California summer air as their lake urged them to join.

Maybe he was finally ready to talk about his dad passing. He hadn't said a word about it since she initially told him in the hospital. "Hey there!" He slowly turned, but he didn't smile.

"Hey." She stepped onto the porch, arranged the second armchair so she could face him, sat in it, and grabbed both of his hands.

She looked past his irises and into his soul while she waited. "I don't know how to tell you."

"Is this about your dad?" She couldn't tell what emotion passed through his gaze. "You haven't said his name for weeks."

"No." She wanted to say something, anything, but it wouldn't have mattered. He had to do this on his own, at his own pace.

"I think you know." She held her breath, building up her walls so that whatever pain would come next, it would not break her. "I am not the same man I was." She sat up straighter and let her diaphragm expand. "The darkness inside me... I can't seem to shake it. It is always there. No matter how much I pray. No matter what I do to get rid of it. The only time I can't see it, I can't feel it, is when I am with you. I was sent to war by God, asked by Him to go serve this country, to serve Him. All I have now is darkness that is eating me from the inside out."

He continued, "I remind myself daily that I killed people. I took the lives of His children, of children He loves. It is one of the worst sins to commit, and I not only did it once, but I did it over and over and over again, love. Why would He send me overseas to murder His children? To commit one of the most abominable sins in His eyes?" Before she could respond, he continued, "I have this recurring dream that just reminds me almost every night of the new me, of the impenetrable darkness inside me. It won't ever go away."

"What happens in the dream?" He relayed the details of his dream from memory.

"So, God is there with you, but you can't see Him?"

"Yes. Every time I think I get just a little closer, but I can never really see Him." She continued to look into the forest of his eyes.

"Maybe you are looking in the wrong place." SJ cocked his head.

"How so?"

"Well, as you know, we cannot see Him with our eyes just yet, but that doesn't mean we can't see Him with our hearts and our minds." He let that sink in. A smile filled his gaze. "Besides, we all have darkness in us. It is a part of the journey, but that is why we strive for more light. We forget that darkness only has as much power over us as we let it, and darkness gives way for more light. It encourages us to be more grateful for the light, for Him."

She squeezed his hand and leaned closer. After leaving a lingering kiss on his forehead, she continued, "Darkness, in all its irony, is a reminder of Him. It is a reminder that while there is darkness in this world, inside you." She raised their hands to his chest. "Inside me." She raised their hands to her chest. "It is so we can more clearly see the good, so we can see Him, even if He isn't physically there. Part of being mortal means we will sin, we will make choices that do not align us with His will, but with His atonement, with His grace and mercy, we can be cleansed. We can see and be His light. Faith, my love, is not just believing in what we can't see, but it is also believing in what He can see."

He shifted his braced leg to extend toward the lake as he found the edge of his chair. As he let himself fall, his lips found hers for several long seconds. He was the one to pull back, but he never let her hands go.

Head bowed, he began, "Father, I thank You for Anja's listening ear; it is one of Your greatest gifts. We thank You that we are here together. We thank You that we are safe. We thank You for being with us no matter what. We thank You for loving us no matter what. We ask You to please continue to be patient with us as we learn to grow closer to You, closer to each other. Please continue to protect us, to protect our loved ones. Please give Mom extra blessings. I know she tries to hide it, but she is still hurting, and only You can give her the peace, the healing, the love that she seeks, so please continue to be with her. Thank You for right now, for this moment, for how happy we are. We love you. In the name of Jesus Christ, amen."

"Amen." Her smile hid her eyes; that was his favorite. "All because of Him." She looked up. At SJ. At their house. At the lake. At His hand all around her. "Because of Him, we live. Because of Him, we smile, laugh, learn, grow." She took her time with each word. "Because of Him, we can love—truly, deeply, passionately love." She kissed the top of his hands. "Because of Him, we have every reason to hope." She kissed him just before folding her legs like a pretzel. Her yellow toenails reflected the sun. "So, how is your team doing?" He held up his finger, leaned toward her, grabbed the bottom lip of the chair, and pulled it toward him.

Once he was satisfied that she was close enough to him, he responded, "As good as they can be. All of us are home for now. Munoz might go back, but he wants more time here. Phillipe just got engaged to his high school sweetheart." His eyebrows folded as something came to the forefront of his memory. "Deeks actually called me the other day. He had questions about a conversation we had a couple weeks before we were rescued."

"What was the conversation about?"

"I don't remember all of the details, but he kept asking me about God." She folded her hands in her lap, all attention on him.

"And what did you say?" A darkness descended into his gaze. She crossed her legs and grew closer to him. "Love, what's wrong?"

"Nothing. I just… I don't remember everything, but I do remember feeling angry. I was angry at God when he asked. I don't think I lied or anything like that, but I am glad he called. I want him to know the truth." He saw the fear he had dreaded would plague her if he mentioned his wavering faith. "Love, please, please don't worry. I promise you that I trust Him. Do I understand everything? No. Do I have all of the answers? No. And that is okay. He does." He smiled as he repeated her words back to her, "And that is all I need to know." She kissed him and let him kiss her back. She prayed for the right moment to tell him, and she had a feeling this was it.

The buzzing of his phone penetrated their moment. Slightly annoyed and tempted to ignore it, since he appeared to take no notice of it, she thought against it until she felt prompted to answer. Floating into the bedroom, she picked up the phone.

"Hello?"

"Hello? Scott?" Trying to contain the anxiety that sprang into her body, she took a deep breath.

"Oh, hello, Master Sergeant Bates! It has been a while." Her tone lightened up. His didn't.

"It is good to hear your voice, Anja, but I am afraid I don't have good news…"

She dropped the phone and froze. He was supposed to make a full recovery. He was supposed to be with his fiancée. But he didn't. And he wasn't.

"Anja?" SJ had bolted to her side once he heard the phone crash to the ground. He placed his arms on her shoulders. "Love, talk to me."

How was she supposed to tell him that his best friend just died? Phillipe, the man who saved him multiple times, the man who listened to him talk about her when no one else would, was gone, and he was not coming back. She definitely couldn't tell him they were going to be parents in less than nine months now.

About the Author

While she is a new author, Kathryn Merriam is not new to writing. From her early years through her college years, she has studied and developed writing skills she hopes to utilize to bring hope and light to a world that seems to be crowded with darkness. Motivated with a love for God and for her family, she dreams big and strives to make a difference. Along with her dog, she lives in California surrounded by family.